BOB PATMORE'S
PERFECT VISION

BOB PATMORE'S PERFECT VISION

by Bob Patmore

Granta Editions

© General Portfolio Management Services Ltd

First published 1991

ISBN 0 906782 589

Published by Granta Editions
47 Norfolk Street, Cambridge, CB1 2LE
Granta Editions is an imprint of The Book Concern Ltd

Design and production in association with
Book Connections, Cambridge

Typeset by Eurotype 2000 Ltd, Hertford

Reproduced, printed and bound in Great Britain by
BPCC Hazell Books
Aylesbury, Bucks, England
Member of BPCC Ltd

A CIP catalogue record for this book is available in The British Library

For my family, friends and colleagues who have all, knowingly or unknowingly, helped me to grow and contributed towards my own Perfect Vision.

CONTENTS

PICTURE CONTENTS

FOREWORD

I first met Bob Patmore during the Hannibal Walk across the French Alps in 1988. Bob walked the 500-mile journey with Ian Botham and, in the process, helped to raise thousands of pounds for Leukaemia Research. Since that time I have had many dealings with him and with General Portfolio, the company which he, Vincent Isaacs and others, have helped to build into a multi-million pound organisation.

When I heard that Bob had decided to write *Perfect Vision*, a book on *'Being the best you can possibly be'*, I was not unduly surprised, for I knew that he had a lot of positive and worthwhile things to say. Nor was I surprised when I learned that all profits from the book would be donated to the Fund. This is just one more example of his generosity and that of his colleagues at General Portfolio.

Our association with the company began with the Botham/Hannibal walk in 1988 and to date has raised in excess of £450,000. The value of such an association in terms of raising money to further research can be seen in the advances which have been made in treating leukaemia over the past 30 years, particularly in children. If, with the aid of companies such as General Portfolio, the pace of developments can be maintained, by the year 2001 we could be close to saving every child who gets this dreadful disease.

Unfortunately, the children who die are those who contract the more complicated or unusual forms of leukaemia and are, therefore, more difficult to treat. Nevertheless, there have been terrific achievements in leukaemia treatment since the 1950s. With the continued support of people like Bob Patmore and their companies, there can be real hope that during the next ten years successful research will extend a far brighter and better future to leukaemia patients of all ages.

Therefore, I have pleasure in being associated with this worthwhile project and, on behalf of the Leukaemia Research Fund, thank you for your support.

Douglas Osborne
Executive Director
Leukaemia Research Fund

– 1 –

PERFECT VISION

How many times has someone looked you straight in the face and said, 'Trust me!' And how many times have you agreed to trust them and it has turned out to be the 'worst decision' you have ever made?

Well, I am going to ask you to trust me. I guarantee that, if you take from this book all the positive changes and developments I outline, not only will you be lifted from your current level of achievement to a pitch of human excellence about which you will only have dreamed, but you will learn truly to trust the one person who will have made it happen – yourself.

Sounds extreme? That is why you should trust me. You cannot say, 'I'm this type of person' or 'I'm that type of person, so Perfect Vision won't work for me'. Whoever you are, you will already, unknowingly, be practising some aspects of Perfect Vision. Indeed, we all do automatically.

Some actions we take, for example, driving a car from one part of the country to another to arrive at an agreed time, involve thousands of decisions, which we seem to take instinctively. Yet these decisions are not instinctive: they are all learned.

'you will already, unknowingly, be practising some aspects of Perfect Vision'

They involve thinking of the best means of reaching your destination, taking in your stride any doubts about your ability to get there, acting upon your plan and maintaining a standard of driving that enables you to arrive safely.

It is a pattern of thought, a programme if you like, that involves harnessing common sense, good habits and application. It can be used for any and every situation you encounter. In this book, I set out the different elements of Perfect Vision, in a series of successive steps, as on a rising staircase, involving four stages summarised as:

*** THINK *** BELIEVE *** ACT *** BECOME ***

At the top of the steps is your own personal summit: that of fulfilling your true potential. I do not need to build the staircase for you, it is already there and you are already on it. My aim is to illuminate the stairs and show where one stage ends and another begins, so that I can help you to the top – to *Being the best you can possibly be*.

In return I ask you to trust me with your time.

HOW DO THEY DO IT?

'there is a formula for being successful and a formula for being unsuccessful'

I am sure that you wonder why some people are successful and others are not – why some people have inexhaustible energy and a love of life, while others seem sluggish and prepared to accept whatever life seems to deal them. The difference has nothing whatsoever to do with their qualifications, their background or their education. It has to do with their vision.

There is a formula for being successful and a formula for being unsuccessful and every one of us possesses the knowledge to follow either. Much of this knowledge lies in common sense, but the fact that so few of us do ourselves justice reveals that this sense is not so common after all.

Using Perfect Vision on the important things in life can mean the difference between success and failure. Those people who have achieved the goals they have set themselves have, either consciously or subconsciously, used Perfect Vision to the full.

I once attempted to make it as a soccer star and, later, as a musician. I never succeeded. Looking back, however, at a financial consultancy which has grown from 400 to over 3,500 in under five years, I can identify a clear change in my thinking over the past decade and a half. I have often likened it to finding a path through a jungle, so much so that I considered calling this book, 'The Law of the Jungle', but that would probably have made Perfect Vision sound more difficult than it really is.

In my opinion all that you need is a proper awareness of Perfect Vision and a positive commitment to practising it. If you have these you will, sooner or later, be successful. Perfect Vision is open to everyone, so long as they understand that it is an extension of the life which they already lead and to be successful they have to take responsibility for creating their own success.

My own use of Perfect Vision has taken me from average achievements in football and music to phenomenal success in a career in financial planning. Not only have I become both financially wealthy and achieved personal happiness but also, in passing on my philosophy, I have had the pleasure of seeing those around me, who have practised it, achieve the personal satisfaction and monetary wealth of their dreams.

I sincerely believe that the ideas in this book will help you to live a happier and more successful life and I wish you every success in the pursuit of your own excellence.

'using Perfect Vision on the important things in life can mean the difference between success and failure'

WHAT IS PERFECT VISION?

VISION : A vivid mental image produced by the imagination

Everyone, without exception, thinks in pictures. When some-one says to you, 'Think of a dog', you do not conjure up in your mind the letters D-O-G. You visualise the animal itself.

Perfect Vision involves what I call 'mindsight', allowing you to picture, in your mind, a clear view of exactly what is to happen in the future. Mindsight enables you to 'see' an object or future event in your mind's eye with complete clarity. You could be seeing yourself being offered a job at an interview, picturing yourself driving a new car, or even visualising something as mundane as owning a new washing machine. All of these involve vision.

'the Think – Believe – Act – Become formula describes the stages we must go through to ensure we attain the result we initially pictured'

Mindsight provides the target and Perfect Vision enables you to take the steps needed to reach it. The **Think – Believe – Act – Become** formula describes the stages we must go through to ensure we attain the result we initially pictured.

Let us take the simple example of that washing machine. Some months ago, I visited my sister to find that she was the proud owner of a new one. In obtaining it she had used Perfect Vision.

She began by thinking about owning a new washing machine. Then she visualised what life would be like with it – probably right down to where it would sit in her kitchen. Then she convinced herself that it was a good idea to buy it. After that, all that was needed was for her to work out the best way for obtaining, buying and bringing it home. Her Perfect Vision became reality.

If we can naturally use Perfect Vision on such a small scale to such good effect, then why do we not use it more often for the important things in life? As you can see, Perfect Vision is simply the combination of experiencing a very real desire and then acting to fulfil that desire.

If we wish to increase our success in life then we must learn to use our vision on the important things. We can all achieve so much more if we are prepared to think 'big' and work hard. It does not matter what level of success in life we have already achieved, there is always room for improvement.

You need to have two key attitudes to be able to use your Perfect Vision to its full potential. The first is to be able always to visualise yourself in the way that you wish to be – not in the way that you are now – and always to make your vision a positive one.

The second is to be prepared to change.

'we can all achieve so much more if we are prepared to think "big" and work hard'

A NEED FOR CHANGE

I am sure that at some time in our lives every one of us has heard someone say that we have potential. I remember feeling vaguely insulted when I heard that being said about me, because I realised that having potential meant that I had not fulfilled it.

Potential before it is realised is like having 9p in a telephone box – you are very close to making something happen, but, unless you take action to change the situation, nothing will ever happen. It is what I call the *nearly* or *almost* syndrome. When I was endeavouring to make a career in football I *nearly* scored a lot of goals and the clubs *nearly* retained me for another season.

I have often likened it to flying in my helicopter and having one digit wrong on the radio frequency. I can shout as loudly as I like but they will not be able to hear me back at air traffic control.

'the only real limits to our success are the limits which we place upon ourselves'

If you nearly achieve something you have not achieved it. You may have only narrowly missed your target, but you have missed it. The experience can be of value only if you learn from it. Indeed, *nearly* doing something, *almost* achieving success, is a cause neither for celebration nor consolation; it should be a cause of inspiration, a spur to dedication and, above all, it should be the reason for examining what faults in our planning, our self-belief, our action or our reaction prevented us, so narrowly, from achieving our goals. For, whatever our aspirations, the major barriers to our success are those we erect ourselves.

Above all, when recognising that we are not where we want to be in life, we need to acknowledge that our current thinking, beliefs and actions will not take us towards our vision and so we must change.

At this point I would stress that reading the rest of this book will be a waste of time unless you are prepared to change. It is designed to help those who want to improve themselves and any improvement programme, in any sphere of life, has to involve the acceptance of change.

A MANUAL FOR LIFE

I have already said that the only real limits to our success are the limits which we place upon ourselves. I will now explain why.

Have you ever considered that whenever you buy something new – a car, a radio, an exercise machine – you are given an instruction manual explaining how to use it properly?

Well, some time ago, the thought occurred to me that we are all born into this world with no ready-made guide for developing our thinking, our sense of self-belief, our motivation for action and our maintenance of standards. In short there is no manual for reaching our full potential, for getting the most out of life.

The only guidance we receive is that we form ourselves from the information provided by those around us and the environment in which we grow; we absorb the teachings of our parents and teachers, who themselves have absorbed the teachings of their parents and teachers, and so on.

I do not apologise for stressing again that we can all achieve much more than we think we can. One of the immediate changes we must make before we can begin to achieve greater results is in our basic thinking. We must be willing to question, layer upon layer, the basic attitudes that have been instilled in us since childhood.

On the following pages, I will outline for you the process involved in the **Think – Believe – Act – Become** formula: a process that has proved so successful, both for myself and for those individuals I have helped to develop.

I have no doubt that when you start to follow the formula completely, altering your thoughts, beliefs, actions and re-actions, you will be on the road to doing yourself justice, to *'Being the best you can possibly be'*.

'when you start to follow the formula completely you will be on the road to being the best you can possibly be'

– 2 –

THINK

'undoubtedly, we are all much better, much more capable than we think we are.'

The most important factor in determining our level of achievement in life is the way in which we think.

Everything we do, every action we take, begins with a preceding thought. Our thoughts determine how we act and how we act determines the results we eventually get. So, if your current thinking is not getting you to where you want to be, then the first thing you must change is the way in which you think.

Undoubtedly, we are all much better, much more capable than we think we are. I am sure we can all think of situations in which we have surprised or excelled ourselves in achieving things which we had not thought were possible. But you should ask yourself why were you surprised? Unquestionably your associates, your environment or, most importantly, you yourself, will have convinced you of your own lack of ability.

It is usually only once we have seen evidence of our success that we think that we can create it. In short, everyone can visualise failure. But Perfect Vision, as the words imply, enables you to visualise success.

Indeed, we are going to look at how to turn around the thought processes that conjure up failure so that we can visualise our goals before having any evidence of our ability to achieve them. We will think that we can do something and will prove ourselves right.

You are probably asking yourself how we are going to achieve this. We can only improve ourselves and our actions if we return to basics and change the thought patterns which we have absorbed since childhood: the thoughts which, from an early age, have been directly influenced by our environment and the people we have contact with.

To achieve new results we must control how we think; we must revert from the automatic thoughts which have been forged over a number of years to the conscious thoughts which will change our approach to life. When we question how we think, why we think in a certain way and the effect that those thoughts have on our daily life then, and only then, can we truly begin the process to become the best person we can possibly be.

'we need to learn to concentrate on the positive and eliminate the negative'

It has been said that our personality and its most basic reactions are forged by whatever we think about most deeply and most often; that if we think about something long enough and act upon those thoughts, it should eventually happen. This is equally true for both good and bad thoughts, so we need to learn to concentrate on the positive and eliminate the negative. Indeed, to be successful we must first think we are successful, believe in that thought and then take the action to ensure that we become successful.

CAUSE AND EFFECT

'if we really want to change our world, the first thing we must change is our mind'

We must always remember that the most important ingredient in our improvement programme is how we think. If we continue to think in the same way that we have always thought then we will continue to achieve the same results. So, if we really want to change our world, the first thing we must change is our mind.

The normal reaction when we are not succeeding at something is to become negative towards the undertaking itself. Not surprisingly, when we are not getting the results we want, we begin to question our ability to be positive. More often than not, however, it is the negative attitude itself that is both the cause of the current position and the block to remedying it.

In order to turn the whole situation around, we need to treat the cause – the thinking – rather than the effect our actions have had. Indeed, I believe that what we view as the external circumstances governing our lives are a mirror image of our thoughts. Our behaviour (and the results it achieves) is entirely governed by the way we think.

Let us assume that you came around to my house yesterday and my 12-year-old daughter walked up to you and kicked you on the leg. That was obviously bad behaviour on her part. She was doing something very wrong. The way that most parents would react would be to smack the child as a punishment. But, instead, ask yourself what was the cause?

In short her bad behaviour would have been caused by her feeling upset about something; feelings that came from the way that she was thinking and the punishment would have made her feel even worse.

The real solution would be to discover how her thinking had

upset her and address it. It would only be by changing the way she thinks and, in turn, feels, that she would be able to change her behaviour for the better.

PRECEDING THOUGHTS

Without exception everything we do starts with a preceding thought. Every action we take is preceded by a conscious or subconscious decision to act – whether opening doors, picking up a book, making a telephone call.

'everything we do starts with a preceding thought'

In order to run a proper improvement programme to upgrade our level of achievement, we have to change and improve the quality of those preceding thoughts.

IT ALL BEGINS AT AN EARLY AGE

The process of how we think all begins at an early age. As children we absorb the ideas and actions of the people around us and are influenced by our environment. But unknowingly, in doing so, we accept the limitations which are placed on us by others.

How many times have you heard someone say, 'I'm not musical' or 'I'm not sports minded', to name but two? When I hear people speak like that, I normally ask them for their reasons for thinking that way and the answer is usually that it lies in something they were told as a child. As we will show in the chapter on belief, if you tell yourself, or are told, something often enough you will eventually believe it.

Thus, instead of finding out for ourselves whether we are capable of achieving more, we accept that what we have been told is true and we do not try. We genuinely think that we are not musical or are not sports minded.

We have to realise that it is our own thoughts that limit our achievements and, in order to improve, we need to adjust the way we think. Personally, I am strongly convinced that anybody who has the desire to succeed, and then works a programme to achieve that success, can gain outstanding results in music, sport or, indeed, any field – providing that they have the absolute yearning to succeed and the right programme to support that desire.

'it is our own thoughts that limit our achievements'

As I said before, the basis for all of our thoughts comes from what we are taught as children. If we are fortunate enough to be brought up in a positive atmosphere, where we are encouraged to think and believe that we can do anything, then we thrive and achieve much more.

Unfortunately, most children are brought up in a negative atmosphere. They are continually told what they cannot do, instead of being allowed to develop along the principle that they just have not learned yet.

Many parents spend the first two years teaching their children to talk, then spend the next few years telling them to be quiet. I am sure we have all heard the phrase, 'Children should be seen and not heard'. Yet, with children having to cope with that kind of contradiction from an early age, they are hardly going to have the best possible start to their development.

'anybody who has the desire to succeed, and then works a programme, can gain outstanding results in any field'

Then the child begins school and is conditioned by the strengths, weaknesses and beliefs of both teachers and schoolfellows and the cycle goes on.

During my school days my one and only interest was football. I paid very little attention to day-to-day school work and used to focus on becoming a better footballer and being the youngest player in the senior team. So, I feel it was inevitable that I should become very good at football whilst my school reports consistently told me that I was getting far from excellent results in the majority of academic subjects.

A few years ago, however, when I decided that I wanted to become a helicopter pilot, I needed to re-learn some of the subjects I had been taught at school – map reading, compasses, meteorology, etc. Had I followed the pattern outlined above and followed the thinking from my school reports, I would have accepted what I had been told and thought that I was no good at Geography. I would never have tried to learn and never would have been successful in obtaining my pilot's licence. So, instead of convincing myself that I could never be good at Geography I told myself that my previous poor performance was merely due to my former lack of interest; and that now the only reason I did not have the knowledge needed was solely because I had not yet learned it.

To raise our children in a positive atmosphere, we need to motivate them to learn. If they continually receive poor school reports, and their parents confirm that they are not academic, they will obviously feel de-motivated and start to think that they are not as 'bright' as other people. Yet, if they are encouraged to think that they are capable, instead of con-tinually being told that they are not, they will be encouraged to build and improve upon the results they have achieved in the past.

'to raise our children in a positive atmosphere, we need to motivate them to learn'

SUCCESS COMES IN CANS, NOT CANNOTS

One of the greatest barriers in any improvement programme is in our thinking as to what we can and cannot do. Anything is possible if it has already been done by someone else. Unfortunately, as I have indicated, adults keep telling children about what they cannot do instead of focusing on what they can. Inevitably the children end up with limited thinking about their capabilities.

'anything is possible if it has already been done by someone else'

How many times have you heard someone say to a child, 'Don't go near the water, you can't swim'. However, it is not that the child cannot swim, merely that he has not yet learned how to

25

swim. Yet, if he is continually told that he cannot swim, he will think that he is incapable of it and will never take the actions required to learn.

In order to progress, we must get across to ourselves that we can do anything if someone has done it before us. We must change our vocabulary from 'I can't' to 'I haven't learned yet'. If we continue to think in negative terms we will never take the steps or actions necessary to turn a 'cannot' into a 'can' and we shall limit our success in life. So, when you find yourself saying, 'I can't run a marathon', 'I can't cook' or 'I can't play the piano', remind yourself that it is not that you cannot. You can. It is just that you have not learned yet!

It is still surprising, however, how many people tell you what they cannot do, as opposed to what they can.

When you ring people within the service industry they, inevitably, start off by telling you what they cannot do. I am sure that we have all had dealings with people who ostensibly wish to supply some sort of service, only to be told that they 'couldn't possibly give an estimate for three weeks' or they 'couldn't possibly start work before a certain date'.

'there is no such concept as cannot'

There is, however, no such concept as cannot. If the desire is great enough, if the job is important enough, then the service will be provided. In most cases, when people tell you that they cannot do something, what they really mean is that they can, but that it is currently not convenient for them.

Whenever I hear someone tell me what they cannot do it reminds me of the occasion when I was due to make an appointment with a knee specialist and was told that I could not have an appointment for three-and-a-half weeks.

I explained to his secretary that I would be in the area the next day and asked whether there was any possible way that she could squeeze me in. She said that it was absolutely impossible.

Then I asked her if she would be very honest with me if I asked a direct question, to which she agreed. I then said, "If Prince Charles needed to see the specialist tomorrow would you find him a slot?"

She replied, "Yes, I suppose I would."

To which I replied, "Good, well he's not coming so I'll take his appointment."

After sharing the joke she agreed to give me an appointment but told me that I would have to wait.

'remember that success comes in cans, not cannots'

This same rule applies to many situations. Take a restaurant as an example. You know that, when they say they are fully booked, if you ask politely and positively they can normally squeeze in another table for four.

People's instant reaction is, 'I can't do that'. Realise that you really can. There is no such thing as cannot. If you ever find yourself thinking, 'I can't', always remember that success comes in cans, not cannots.

DEVELOPING OUR THOUGHT PROCESSES

Have you ever wondered why it is that one man is happy while another is unhappy? Why one man is poor and another is rich or one is positive and another is negative? After all, we are all born with brains of approximately the same size. But the answer lies not in what we have, but in how we use it and with what we programme it.

Just imagine, for a moment, that your mind is like a computer. As children we are born with a blank disc which, from the very first day, is immediately fed with information by our parents, our teachers, our environment. As we grow older we become responsible for the data we allow to be processed, but, instead of taking control and deciding upon the value of each piece of information, we still allow outside influences to govern our thinking.

As children we have little control over the thoughts that are, consciously or subconsciously, planted in our minds; absorbing information without questioning its value has become a habit by the time we are adults.

'never underestimate the power of our subconscious mind'

For most people, the subconscious mind has no filter on it and it will process whatever information it is fed. I am sure that we all remember how, as children, we struggled before we went to sleep to remember a poem we were due to recite the next day and yet awoke to find ourselves word perfect. That is because our subconscious mind worked on it overnight.

We must, therefore, never underestimate the power of our subconscious mind. We must at all times feed it positive thoughts so that it can go to work on achieving the required results.

MAKE THE END JUSTIFY THE MEANS

Many statements we make from habit are very often untrue and/or negative. We use phrases like, 'I am too old', 'too young', 'the wrong colour', 'too fat', 'too thin', etc. These statements work totally against us. They stop us taking actions before we even start.

Yet, we can make this principle work for us rather than against us. If we have to make statements from habit, instead of using negative statements let us use positive ones. We should be machiavellian and 'make the end justify the means'.

Where, before, we generalised on negative things, let us now generalise on the positive. When you find yourself thinking, 'I am too old', think of people like Colonel Sanders, Walt Disney and Ronald Reagan, all of whom made a tremendous impact later in life. Think of all the experience you have now which you can turn to your advantage.

'ask yourself whether your thoughts are productive and constructive or non-productive and destructive'

In order to improve our level of success we have to take charge of our thought processes. We have to go back to basics and question each piece of information we programme into our minds. So keep asking yourself whether your thoughts are productive and constructive or non-productive and destructive.

FEED YOUR MIND

It is funny how some people think themselves heroes if they have missed their lunch and others set such store by it that they take their break at a certain time.

I am not saying that there is anything wrong with this, but it seems by our attitude that feeding our stomachs is generally of much more importance than feeding our minds.

Yet, it is not our stomachs that make the important decisions in day-to-day life. It is not our stomachs which will map and plan out our complete future. It is our thought processes which will determine how far we will succeed.

'concentrate on punching in positive encouraging information rather than allowing in negative thoughts'

We feed our stomach three times a day, but how many times do we feed our brain and with what? Because we tend consistently to feed our brains with the wrong 'food' for success, we have to examine what goes into them from both internal and external sources.

We very often blame our environment for our thought patterns and negative thinking, but the majority of the input comes from ourselves and, provided we ensure that it is positive, we cannot fail to improve.

We must, therefore, wash away all the rubbish and negative thoughts from our minds in a similar way to washing dirt from our hands and close our ears to anything which is not going to make us successful.

Negativity will always be around us, but if we concentrate on punching in positive encouraging information, rather than allowing in negative thoughts, we will definitely begin to see a change in our performance. We need to get into the habit of reading Positive Mental Attitude (PMA) books and mixing and talking with successful people. By doing this it will ensure that we are on the right mental diet for success.

A POSITIVE MENTAL ATTITUDE

You may have heard it said that 95% of people are negative and 5% are positive. However, I believe that within that 5% there is another 95% and 5%; and within that 5% there is another 95% and 5% and so on. It is all a matter of levels.

Being positive is easy when things are going well and you are successful but so much harder when things are going badly. When things are not so good and tough times appear, that is when we need a positive mental attitude most of all. However, it is at the very time that we need it most that it tends to elude us.

It is quite usual to follow the route that when things are good we walk around looking like we have swallowed a coat-hanger and when things are bad we look like we have just lost a pound and found a sixpence.

To be successful, you need to step out of the crowd and not do what usual people do. Always remind yourself that unusual people do unusual things, get unusual results and, indeed, can earn unusual money.

When things are going badly, when we are not achieving what we want to achieve, it is too easy to slip into negative thought patterns. So remember, the formula for success is that, when things are going well, you need to think positively and when things are going badly, think doubly positively. I am sure you will agree that this is the only way of turning things around.

'unusual people do unusual things, get unusual results and, indeed, can earn unusual money'

WHAT DO YOU FOCUS ON?

There are always different ways of looking at any situation and we will normally see what we expect. The reason why most people do not get to where they want to be in life is because they focus on the negative, on what could go wrong.

I was returning recently from a business trip on a non-stop flight from Hong Kong to London Heathrow. While visiting the flight deck I struck up a conversation with the pilot who told me that we would have burned 154 tonnes of fuel by the time we landed at Heathrow, but, even so, would still have half an hours fuel left. I kept thinking about how incredible it was that an aeroplane could get off the ground with all that fuel; plus the luggage, the weight of the aircraft itself and the passengers.

'the reason why most people do not get to where they want to be in life is because they focus on the negative'

The more I thought about it, the more I was impressed, not only with the modern technology behind the invention itself, but also with the brilliance of the thinking by the individuals behind its conception.

On landing at Heathrow, I mentioned this to the friend who was meeting me. I asked him if he knew how much fuel we had used between Hong Kong and London and he admitted that he did not. With my mind still focused on my vision of the designers and the creative thinking which had brought about the plane's invention I told him. Yet, instead of sharing my positive thoughts, his immediate reaction was, 'My God, no wonder they make so much mess when they crash. No wonder they burst into flames.' His comment made me realise just how very differently we all think because of the nature of our thought processes themselves.

FOCUS ON THE POSITIVE

I am sure we have all heard sayings like, 'Two people behind bars. One sees mud, the other sees stars', or been asked the question about whether a glass is half-empty or half-full.

When we mention ideas to people, the majority of them automatically think in the negative. They think of all the reasons for 'why not', instead of all of the reasons for 'why'. But, if we continually focused on the negative we would never do anything in life.

On my helicopter there are a series of lights to warn the pilot should anything be malfunctioning during the flight. There is one red light that, when illuminated, indicates engine failure – something which both my passengers and I would take pretty seriously!

When I am flying, however, what I actually do is stare at where I am going and glance at the warning lights. If I stared at the lights and only glanced at where I was going I would never get airborne.

Yet, I have met so many people in life who fail to take off because they focus on all the things that could possibly go wrong, rather than focusing on achieving and developing.

'make sure that you focus on what you want out of life, where you are going and what you want to achieve'

We must not continue to focus on the negative, otherwise it will stop us from taking those first important steps. Make sure that you focus on what you want out of life, where you are going and what you want to achieve, rather than focusing on what could possibly go wrong.

PROBLEMS? – OR JUST SITUATIONS AND SOLUTIONS

To be successful, to improve ourselves, we have to get into the habit of looking for the good in every situation. Negative people approach any difficulty as though it is an overwhelming misfortune that only happens to them, while positive people always approach any difficulties with the thought that there is always a solution.

'get into the habit of saying to yourself, "There's an interesting challenge"'

To succeed in life, we have to get into the habit of seeing any difficulties not as problems, but as situations and challenges.

From a very early stage in my life I was told that problems and progress come hand in hand, but then I realised that there are no such things as problems, merely situations to which there are always solutions.

When something you do not like comes up, get into the habit of saying to yourself, 'There's an interesting challenge.' Focus on the solution rather than the difficulty and you will find out that you are more capable than you thought you were.

On any self-improvement programme you will never ever develop and improve without experiencing difficulties and challenges, so make sure that you are 'solution conscious' not 'problem conscious'.

HOW TO STAY POSITIVE

'make sure that you are "solution conscious" not "problem conscious"'

We often hear people say, 'Avoid the negative', 'Don't mix with people who have negative thoughts' and, indeed, 'Don't mix with people who are less positive than yourself'. But, if we followed that formula, we would eventually have no one with whom to talk and life would be very lonely indeed.

There is negative and positive in everyone and it is up to us not to allow any negative influence to affect who we are and what we become. We need constantly to check on our levels of positiveness. Keep asking yourself, 'Did I react negatively today? Did I even think negatively today? Did I focus on the problem rather than the solution?'

Just remember, every time that something you do not want happens, keep telling yourself that everything happens for a

reason. Keep punching in the point that every adversity carries the seed of greater benefit. Always remind yourself that we do not grow without experience.

If things do not go as you want the natural response is to start thinking negatively. Do not allow yourself to do this. Remember that if you have even one negative thought you should get into the habit of flooding it with ten positives. When our mind is full of positive thoughts there is absolutely no room for negative thinking.

Keep reminding yourself that constructive thinking creates success and that negative thinking is destructive: it causes fear and worry. It will not help you to overcome any difficulties. There is only one way forward and that is to think positively at all times.

'keep reminding yourself that constructive thinking creates success'

FACE YOUR FEARS

Just as one of people's greatest fears is of failure, so one of the greatest causes of failure is fear. Most fears are caused by lack of understanding. The more we understand the less we fear and the less we understand the more we fear.

As children we used to be frightened of ghosts, the bogey man, the dark, and our imagination fed those fears until we were sure in our minds that they were fact. This only goes to prove the power of the mind.

Fear is extremely destructive and has to be removed. It is a self-imposed barrier against developing our thoughts, preventing us from getting what we want out of life. The longer we allow fear to fester, the worse it will become, so we must analyse it, understand it and take heavy action to cure it.

To overcome our fears we need to be specific about their causes. Very often people mislead themselves about what they actually fear, but we need to recognise the real cause so that we can take action to deal with it.

'the only way to overcome our fear is to face it.'

We all have fears but most of them are false. One of the many fears that people admit to experiencing is that of flying. Yet, it is not flying that they fear, it is the thought of crashing.

The only way to overcome our fear is to face it. The more quickly we take action to remove the fear, the more quickly the fear will disappear. But how do we press ourselves into action? By asking specific questions, for example, 'Can I live the rest of my life without overcoming this fear?'

If we do not deal with the fear immediately it will grow and get a grip on us. If we allow our fears continually to stop us from taking action they will stop us from becoming the complete person we are more than capable of being.

So we must not allow our fears to grow. We must face them head on. We will then suddenly realise that we are beginning to develop as a superior person through the very fact of eliminating the fear that has held us back in the past.

I continually meet people who are living their lives with the pain of fear, rather than with the pleasure of having overcome their fears. Instead of dwelling on the fear, dwell on the problems it will cause you to retain it. Look at the benefits that removing the fear will have and focus on those.

'do what you fear most and your fear will disappear'

Remember that you are more than capable of overcoming your fears and that, by overcoming them, you will have grown as an individual; you will have added value to yourself as a human being. Do what you fear most and your fear will disappear.

WHY WORRY

I have met people who worry about absolutely everything in life. I have even met people who worry because they are not worried about something.

Most worries are caused by indecision. We worry after an event or after making a decision, but that is surely the wrong time. The time to fully apply yourself is before you make any decision.

Life is so busy that, if you spend your time thinking about past problems, you will be overcome by the current ones so, when a situation comes along ask yourself, 'If I worry about this will it improve the situation?' The answer will obviously be 'no', because worry only escalates negative thinking and, as we already know, negative thinkers get negative results which means that you will start to worry again.

So, if you find yourself worrying about anything, try this little exercise. Tell yourself that you are not allowed to worry about anything for more than ten seconds and that if after that time you are still alive then you have got nothing to worry about.

Another major cause of worry is when people talk about us. We get worried and concerned, if people speak behind our backs. Yet, the most criticised people in the country are always also the most successful and prominent so, if you really want to concern yourself, worry that someone is not talking about you.

On your road to *'Being the best you can possibly be'* make sure that you are continually controlling your thoughts and thinking positively about what you can do by removing fear and worry from your life.

'tell yourself that you are not allowed to worry about anything for more than ten seconds and that if after that time you are still alive then you have got nothing to worry about'

KEY POINTS TO PERFECT VISION

> ▶ Always think positively
>
> ▶ Treat the cause not the effect
>
> ▶ Get into the habit of mixing with successful people and reading PMA books
>
> ▶ Be solution conscious, not problem conscious
>
> ▶ Take heavy action to remove fear
>
> ▶ Do not worry

STEVE PERRYMAN

"The biggest influence is your parents. When I decided to go into football my parents were 100% behind me. They said if you really want to do it, go and do it. My family was a very positive influence. I think that if my parents had not been behind me then I would probably have backed off. There would have been too much against me as a 15 year old."

ALLISON FISHER

"You get to fear losing if you think about things too much, so you've just got to have really positive thoughts. Some days I play so badly that I wonder if I'm ever going to play well again. But then you get back to the table and hit a good patch and you know it's there. I think that 90% of the game is in the head."

FRANK BRUNO

"You really have got to want to win and believe you can win. If you get into the ring thinking you will lose, you already have. Very often, the only thing which keeps a boxer going in a tough fight is his belief in himself. If you can knock out your own negative thoughts, you have already won half the battle."

JOHN BARNES

"I was always told that I could do things. I think that is what my parents built into me. But, if they had told me that it was the other way around I would not have attempted them in the first place."

38

– 3 –

BELIEVE

The single most important ingredient that all achievers have in common is their belief in themselves.

If you study successful people you realise that they do not necessarily have more qualifications than anybody else, nor have they gone to a better school nor had a better background. They are actually ordinary people who have developed a lot of belief in themselves and have acted upon that belief. They have stretched their minds to allow themselves to believe that they can achieve anything and have consistently told themselves that they can achieve and will achieve. Inevitably, they have achieved.

The difference between achievers and non-achievers is that achievers believe that they create whatever happens in their life; that nothing is down to luck.

In order to be successful, we have to dispel the superstitions of the past. We have to believe that we control whatever happens to us and that we can change life for the better. We have to believe that it is possible for each and every one of us to make a difference to someone else's life.

'achievers believe that they create whatever happens in their life'

THE POWER OF SELF-BELIEF

'the power of belief in yourself is the difference between success and failure'

There are many ingredients in the formula to help you succeed in life but none is more important than self-belief. The power of belief in yourself is the difference between success and failure. There will always be those around you who will try to make you question your ability to achieve your goal, but they cannot hold you back if you really believe in yourself.

There are many stories which illustrate the power of self-belief but none is more remarkable than the story of 'The Miracle Man'.

On 10th March 1981, businessman Morris Goodman left his home on a pleasure trip in his private plane. On its approach to the landing strip, the aircraft crashed and Mr Goodman sustained extensive injuries which should have killed him.

'Morris Goodman believed that he could beat the odds against him providing he did not accept the negative prognosis of the doctors'

He was admitted to hospital with his neck broken in two places; the first and second cervical vertebrae. The doctor told his family that had he survived with only one break of that magnitude he would have made medical history. His spinal column had been crushed, he had permanent nerve damage causing a dysfunction of the liver, bladder and kidneys; as well as nerve damage to the diaphragm which meant that he would never be able to breathe on his own. His larynx was damaged so badly that if he lived he would never speak again and the injuries sustained to his swallowing reflexes meant that he would never be able to eat or drink normally. Morris Goodman was not expected to survive the night.

The medical profession, however, had not taken into account Mr Goodman's power of self-belief. He knew that, although we are born to win, society conditions us to lose and that our thoughts are a self-fulfilling prophecy. He believed that he could beat the odds against him and walk out of the hospital on his own two feet, providing he did not accept the negative prognosis of the doctors. He set himself the long-term goal of walking out of the hospital on a specific date and began to work towards achieving his goal.

Morris Goodman believed, in his heart and mind, that he would and could be normal again. He ignored the negative influences around him, which were telling him that his goal was impossible, and concentrated on visualising himself off the respirator and walking. He created in his mind a detailed picture of his success and what his life would be like after his goal had been achieved, then set to work on achieving the 'smaller' goals which were the stepping stones to his success.

He taught himself to breathe without the respirator, despite being told that it was impossible. He learned how to talk with the aid of a ping-pong ball placed over his trachea and he taught himself to swallow food and drink normally, in spite of being told that he would choke to death.

Before he left the hospital to which he had originally been admitted, he sent a message to the surgeon to tell him that he would come back and visit him; that he would walk into the doctor's office and shake him by the hand. Eight months after the air crash Morris Goodman did just that.

Had Mr Goodman accepted what the medical profession had honestly believed, he would probably have died or, at best, still been lying in hospital, unable to breathe without aid, unable to eat and unable to talk. But instead of believing in the doctors he believed in himself. He kept telling himself that he would recover, that he would eventually walk out of the hospital and that he would live a normal life again. The combined power of his vision and his belief enabled him to recreate his world.

'the combined power of Morris Goodman's vision and his belief enabled him to recreate his world'

41

WHEN THOUGHT BECOMES BELIEF

The major difference between a thought and a belief is once again one of levels. Our thoughts, the preceding thoughts which go before any action we take, are still somewhat vague messages. They allow us to think, 'I might score a goal' or, 'I might be able to play the piano well'. Yet, the thoughts themselves do not create the belief.

The belief itself comes from a clearer visualisation of that achievement. It comes either from us constantly telling ourselves or being told that we can achieve our goal, or from experiencing the achievement of the goal itself.

Consider the case of the Bumble Bee. Under the laws of aerodynamics it should, theoretically, not be possible for a Bumble Bee to fly – its wings are far too small for the size of

its body. They do fly, however, so why is this? They fly because no one has told them that they cannot. As long as they think and believe that they can, they will continue to do so.

It is much easier, of course, to believe in something once you have done it; and not nearly so easy beforehand. We have seen, in the chapter on thinking, how being constantly told what we cannot do leads us to thinking that we are incapable. The truth is that after being told something consistently, over a period of time, we not only think that we cannot achieve but genuinely believe it.

I am sure that as children we all told white lies. If, however, you continue to tell the same story over and over again then after a little while the line between what is true and what is false disappears. You eventually end up believing in that story. It is like a kind of hypnosis.

BELIEVE IN YOURSELF

To become successful, to achieve our goals, we have to use that hypnosis on ourselves. We have to keep telling ourselves that we can be successful. We have to keep visualising that success in our mind and keep punching in the message that we can achieve it. If we tell ourselves, or are told, something often enough then we will eventually believe in it. One of the keys is to make sure that you never lose faith in yourself. Nothing matters providing you do not lose that belief.

'one of the keys is to make sure that you never lose faith in yourself'

Kevin Keegan tells a story of the day when, as a young Liverpool player, he was due to face the West Ham side which contained three members of the World-Cup-winning squad. His manager was Bill Shankly, renowned as one of the best motivators of men. Shankly's strength was his ability to get his players to believe in themselves and to believe that they were better than any opposition.

Keegan was to be marked by Bobby Moore, widely regarded as one of the best players in the world and, before the match, Shankly singled Keegan out. He made a point of telling Keegan that he had seen Bobby Moore and he looked terrible, he looked old and haggard, was limping and even had dandruff.

Obviously Shankly told Keegan this story to give him much more belief in himself, so that he would have more confidence during the game. Liverpool were the eventual winners, winning 3-1, with Keegan scoring one of the goals. After the match Shankly again approached him and placing his arm around his shoulders, proceeded to tell him that he had scored against one of the best players ever.

Before the game Shankly had told Keegan that he was great and after the game he confirmed it.

This is exactly what we have to do for ourselves if we are to succeed in any improvement programme. We have to keep telling ourselves that we can achieve our goals, that we can be successful.

'mix with people who have achieved something and keep telling yourself that if they can, so can you'

We have to get out of the habit of putting ourselves down in thoughts, words and actions. We have to build our confidence and believe in ourselves. Do not listen to the negative influences of non-achievers around you. Mix with people who have achieved something and keep telling yourself that if they can, so can you.

DO NOT RELY ON LUCK

I am sure that you have noticed that when people are successful in life other individuals make comments like, 'He was just lucky' or 'She was in the right place at the right time'. This also works in the reverse when things do not work out. People comment that, 'He was just unlucky, that's all'.

Yet, look at any individual who has ever made it in life – someone who has achieved outstanding results in sport, become a master craftsman, been successful in business – were they just lucky?

Very early in my career I realised that 'luck' equals 'labour under constructive knowledge' and that if you work very, very hard at something, with a lot of technique and application, you will succeed. You can call it luck, if you like, but I will not.

I do not believe in luck – either good or bad. I believe that everything happens because we create different situations and opportunities and because we believe that we can achieve success.

However, it is absolutely incredible how many lives are ruled by a belief in good and bad luck. Think of the number of people who pick up a daily paper or a magazine to read their horoscopes and then genuinely believe that everyone born under the same star sign will share their fortunes that day. They believe and allow their lives to be ruled by these predictions.

Equally incredible is the amount of faith which we place in superstitions that have been handed down over the years. Ask yourself why should walking under ladders, Friday the 13th and breaking mirrors bring bad luck while horseshoes, four-leaf clovers and black cats bring good luck?

It must be clear to you by now that these objects have no power other than the belief we invest in them.

On one occasion, during my career in football, our coach was delayed and we arrived at the ground about ten minutes before kick-off. We were hurriedly getting changed when the bell went to tell us to get out onto the pitch. As we were leaving, one of the players realised that he had a gaping hole in his sock. We all waited while he hurriedly had another pair given

'if you work very, very hard at something, with a lot of technique and application, you will succeed'

to him from the skip which, obviously, meant he was the last player to put his socks on. That day he had a tremendous game.

During the following weeks he made a point of putting his socks on last, because he believed that by doing so he would have a better game. However, his ability as a footballer had not changed, it was his confidence and belief.

'I thoroughly believe that, if you follow the ideas put to you in this book, within weeks you will discover a noticeable improvement'

I thoroughly believe that, if you follow the ideas put to you in this book, within weeks you will discover a noticeable improvement. But just imagine what would happen if you went home tonight with these wonderful constructive ideas for personal development but inadvertently broke a mirror on your way. Are you really going to try to convince me that the game is up for the next seven years?

With thinking and believing working for us, not against us, we can get away from relying on inanimate objects, talismans and negative thinking.

With positive thinking and total belief in yourself, I really believe that you are on the road to achieving outstanding results.

KEY POINTS TO PERFECT VISION

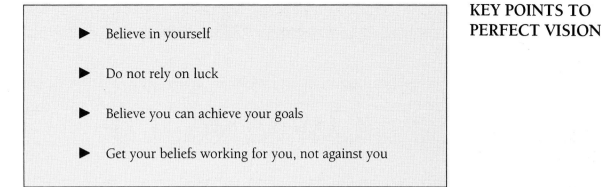

- ▶ Believe in yourself

- ▶ Do not rely on luck

- ▶ Believe you can achieve your goals

- ▶ Get your beliefs working for you, not against you

"I have always had confidence about sport. Life takes a little bit more learning about, but you should never, ever lose the confidence in your own ability. A lot of professionals start changing things and doing things because they are given advice. Everybody will give you advice, particularly when you are not going well, but you can actually get caught in a web and get totally confused. As long as you believe in yourself, and are selective in the advice you take, it does not do any harm to listen."

IAN BOTHAM

"I went through a three-year stint of being unbeaten in the ladies' game, so I was at my peak of confidence. But now the competition's getting better, I'm losing a couple of times and, because I am used to winning, that's hit me harder. So now I have got to learn ways of dealing with it and improving my confidence. You have to have that little bit more. That's what separates people like Steve Davis and Stephen Hendry. They practise hard, they've got talent, but they have got that something extra, that in-built confidence. You've really got to believe in yourself."

ALLISON FISHER

"I am quite positive in my outlook on life. I always think that everything will be okay, no matter what has happened before. There are times when you play a match and you have a bad game, but I look back on all the good times and tell myself that I am a good player, that it has got to come right in the next match. Obviously I doubt myself but, as soon as that starts to happen, you say okay, I know what I have done in the past, what I have achieved and what I know about myself. I am going to make up my own mind about myself."

JOHN BARNES

– 4 –

OWNING UP

*'once we truly
know what we
want we create a
burning desire
that propels us
towards
achieving our
goals'*

If we are all honest with ourselves, every one of us can do better, whatever we have achieved in life and whatever level of success we have attained. In a dynamic world even the most successful have constantly to improve the way that they approach even those challenges they have been mastering every day for years, just to maintain their success.

You may have heard the old saying, 'Be very careful of what you want because you are sure to get it'. The key point to remember from the chapters on thinking and believing is that we can all achieve so much more. But, in order to achieve more, we have to be honest enough with ourselves not to settle for second best.

It is critically important that we are totally honest about what we want out of life. Once we truly know what we want, we create a burning desire that propels us towards achieving our goals. There will be little or no point in moving on to the next chapter, on Goals and Goal Planning, if you are not sufficiently honest with yourself to be able to set proper targets at which to aim. So, before going any further, ask yourself what you really want.

It is not easy. You must be absolutely straight with yourself and know all your strengths and weaknesses – far more difficult to judge in yourself than in other people – in order that you can be totally fair to yourself about what you can become. When doing this it is well worth remembering that, because of the way in which we have been conditioned to think in the past, we tend to set our sights considerably lower than we should. So you need to be willing to look past that conditioning and be ready to see whole areas of your life in a new light.

Keep making checks on yourself. Ask yourself, 'What do I want to be?', 'What do I want to achieve?', 'What would I like to own?' Do not fight the things that you really want. Life is not a rehearsal. If you really want something, at least admit it. Only then will you be able to do something about achieving it. If you only had seven days to live you would be very honest with yourself. Do not wait until then, start now.

'do not fight the things you really want. Life is not a rehearsal'

You are in control of what happens to you. You can decide which people and what parts of your environment you allow to influence the way in which you think and act. Do not allow your mind to keep wandering back to what you used to achieve. The past does not equal the future; the future is dynamic, so must you be. Above all, be honest with yourself. If you are not getting where you want to go, then ask yourself, 'What changes do I need to make to get the results I want?'

'ask yourself "What changes do I need to make to get the results I want?"'

If things are not going your way, be honest enough to admit the truth: that the original desire is still there and that in order to reach your long-term destination you may need a short-term change of direction.

Learn to compensate for any difficulties and do not allow conflict into your mind by telling yourself that you did not want to achieve the results in the first place. If you are totally honest with yourself you will know that there is no easy route to success. It takes a considerable amount of hard work.

CONFLICT AND JUSTIFICATION

The day I started upon the road to success was the day I decided exactly what it was that I wanted out of life – and exactly what I did not.

'the first step in becoming totally honest with yourself is to rid your mind of any conflict'

The first step in becoming totally honest with yourself is to rid your mind of any conflict. Conflict is caused when we are not single-mindedly committed to our desires. Our vision becomes blurred; instead of allowing our mind to focus on achieving our aim, we occupy it with unravelling the conflict between what we are trying to achieve and our ready-made excuses for failure.

Take as an example someone who smokes. The fact is that there is no long-term positive benefit in smoking; it can cause cancer, killing on average 301 people a day in England and Wales. But, instead of making the decision to give up smoking based on that knowledge, people fall into the trap of being dishonest with themselves and then justifying it.

They punch in messages such as, 'My grandfather is 70 years old and has been smoking all his life' or 'I've been smoking for over ten years and it has not done me any harm'. Instead of focusing on their real desire to give up and taking immediate action to achieve it, they allow these excuses firstly to blur that focus and then to become the justification for their lack of success.

'smoking kills on average 301 people a day in England and Wales'

People can also be dishonest when they look at other people's success. Consider how many times you have heard phrases such as, 'Money is the root of all evil' or 'There's more to life than money', and consider who you have heard using those phrases.

I would suggest that in the majority of cases, what people are doing is actually justifying their lack of money. I personally feel that it is the lack of money that causes the greater difficulty; for example, do you ever hear of multi-millionaires mugging little old ladies on the streets? You do not, because they obviously have no need to.

Certainly there is far more to life than money, but again my personal view is that money gives you options and you can do more with it than without it. Some people with money, however, are unhappy, but it is not the money itself that has made them so: it is either because they lack a goal in their lives or because their pursuit of money has made them sacrifice things which they later feel are more important than monetary reward – ie. they have not properly defined their true goals.

'there is far more to life than money'

Another phrase which I often hear is that, 'Success cost him his marriage'. Once again, this is not true. I am sure that you would agree that if he had selected the right partner and taken the right action a successful career would only have enhanced the marriage, not ruined it.

One of the most common phrases used by less successful salesmen to justify a colleague's greater success is, 'He's a born salesman'. A born salesman? Have you ever been to a hospital where newborn babies have identity tags on their wrists that read, 'Salesman born'? Of course salesmen are not born, they are taught, just like other professionals.

'we need to go through a long and hard process to obtain the results we really want'

All of the above are classic justifications that we might use to explain why we are not where we would really like to be. We seek justification for being in our current position, rather than admitting that, in order to achieve success, we need to go through a long and hard process to obtain the results we really want.

ARE WE HONEST ONLY WHEN IT SUITS US TO BE?

At this point in the chapter you need to ask yourself, 'Who is the person about whom I think the most?' Even the most selfless must spend most of their time thinking for themselves and about themselves, even if they have the most uneventful of days.

The fact is that, just to exist, everyone has to be very, very important to himself or herself. You do, whether you admit it to yourself or not, consider every situation you encounter from the viewpoint of how it will directly affect your life.

Let me illustrate this by telling you about a survey which was carried out a few years ago to discover which salary level people considered reasonable for the payment of the higher rate of income tax. The first group questioned were all earning between £7,000 and £10,000 per annum: they believed that the higher rate of tax should come into force at £12,000. The next group were earning between £10,000 and £15,000 per year; they suggested £20,000. The third and final group questioned were all earning between £20,000 and £25,000 per year and they suggested that £30,000 would be a reasonable level.

So, if we are honest with ourselves, we must admit that our view of what is right and fair is tailored to our circumstances.

Let us take another example. Supposing for a moment that a former Master of Foxhounds had the misfortune to come back to life as a fox; do you believe that in that case he would be in favour of fox-hunting? Similarly, consider that in one life you had run a chicken takeaway business but in the next came back as a chicken; how would you view your former business? I do not doubt that there would have been a swift change of view in both cases!

'if we are honest with ourselves, our view of what is right and fair is tailored to our circumstances'

DEALING HONESTLY WITH OTHERS

It is only when we have learned to acknowledge that whatever happens in life will be viewed from whatever point of view that suits us best – that the importance we place on events is directly in proportion to the genuine effect that it will have on our world – that we can begin to understand how essential it is to 'go around to the other side of the table' when dealing with other people and consider any given action from both sides.

When making decisions which affect others ask yourself, 'Would I like to receive what I am giving out?' If you are the boss and you want to ensure that the deal you are offering your employee is fair, then imagine that you are on the employee's side of the table and think about how you would react if it was being offered to you. This is what I call the boomerang effect.

'would I like to receive what I am giving out?'

If you would accept it then give it out. If you would not like to receive it then do not throw it.

If you are totally honest then you will treat people as you would like to be treated.

'treat people as you would like to be treated'

BEING HONEST IN WHAT YOU SAY

Whenever you make a statement, either to other people or yourself, keep running checks to make sure that what you say misleads neither them nor you yourself.

I continually get calls from companies offering their services and claiming that my sales force would make more sales if they attended one of their seminars. During one such call I asked the caller why, if they had all of the answers to making more sales, were they not out selling rather than running one-day seminars. I pointed out that they would make a lot more money if they were selling rather than running courses. When he answered, 'The money is not important', I replied, 'Good, I'll send my sales force to your seminar free of charge'. As you can imagine, his statement was quickly retracted.

'how many times have you heard a salesman say that he is not trying to sell you anything?'

This is a prime example of someone not being honest in what they say. I had heard what he had said, but it was not what he really meant.

Ask yourself how many times you have heard a salesman say that he is not trying to sell you anything. Yet, if he were being honest he would admit that that is exactly what he is trying to do. Certainly, there is nothing wrong with him trying to do his job but, personally, I feel he would be much more successful if he was honest in his approach. The minute he tells me a lie he is misleading me and destroying the trust he needs to create in order to complete the sale.

Again, I had heard what he said, but it was not what he meant.

We also have to be very honest in what we say to ourselves. When we say, 'I'm sorry I was late, it was unavoidable', we are not being honest. If the appointment had been important enough and we had really wanted to be there then we would have done whatever was necessary to ensure that we arrived on time. Very few of us miss the plane for our holidays; it is important to us – and I am sure if someone told you that you had to be at the local town hall to receive a cheque for £250,000 by 12 noon, but that if you arrived late the cheque would be invalid, you would not be late.

Whenever anybody comes out with an ambiguous statement, then the phrase that I usually say to myself is, 'I've heard what you said, but what do you really mean?' I am sure that the more successful people you meet, the more you will notice that high achievers are very direct and honest in their approach, both towards you and towards themselves. They will not have fallen into any of the categories we have discussed here.

'I've heard what you said, but what do you really mean?'

IT IS EASIER TO CRITICISE THAN TO ACHIEVE

Top professionals are criticised every single day both by individuals and by the media. Politicians and journalists are abused and top sportsmen are even taken to task by their own 'fans'.

Once, during my career in football, I went up to take a corner and as I was placing the ball one of our 'fans' decided to tell me what he thought of me. I replied, 'You may think me stupid, but you paid to get into the ground to watch me'.

Again, when I was a musician, I used to criticise records that got into the charts. However, if I had spent more time studying other musicians' achievements and less time looking for things to criticise, then I undoubtedly would have had more success in the music business.

The fact remains that it is much easier to pass judgement than to achieve the results you want. Do not spend time criticising others. The energy and time we waste on doing that would be better spent in growing and developing to achieve our own personal goals.

'do not spend time criticising others'

BEING HONEST ABOUT OUR WEAKNESSES AND OUR STRENGTHS

In any improvement programme we obviously need to highlight the areas which particularly need work and total honesty is vitally important to do that.

One of the reasons why people are not successful in their lives is that they skip through life continually doing the things that they are good at and ignoring the things that they have not yet learned to do. But, in order to improve, you need to become uncomfortable by working on your weaknesses in the company of someone who is far superior in the area you need to improve.

After I had obtained my pilot's licence I wanted to improve my flying. To establish my weaknesses, I ran a checklist on myself to find out the areas I believed were in need of improvement. Then I asked a pilot who had many more hours of flying experience than myself to criticise my weaknesses, to see whether he agreed about the areas that needed to be improved.

'successful people do the little things that unsuccessful people think are unimportant'

By doing this, I removed the conflict in my mind about the specific areas for improvement and all I then had to do was run an improvement programme.

Remember that successful people do the little things that unsuccessful people think are unimportant and that it is the little difference that makes the big difference.

When you are honest enough to know what you want and honest enough to list the weaknesses that need to be changed into strengths, make sure that you find the right person from whom to invite criticism. Ask yourself, 'If I were he, how would I be?', 'If I were she, how would I be?' If you respect them and they are greatly your superior in the area you wish to improve, then ask them whether they agree with you on the improvement programme that you should be running.

A major point here is that you should stay positive by also listing your strengths. As a weakness becomes a strength, move it across the page until all your weaknesses in that area have been removed. Do not forget that weaknesses in our performance are like pregnancy. They grow until they are very evident!

TAKING THE CREDIT AND THE BLAME

Isn't it strange that we often hear people say, 'I'm a self-made success', but never hear anyone say, 'I'm a self-made failure'. It is incredible, but when people fail, it always seems to be someone else's fault.

When being honest with ourselves, we have to learn to take the credit and the blame for everything and anything that happens to us in life. Only then will we realise that everything that happens to us is our responsibility.

'take the credit and the blame for everything and anything that happens to us'

A while ago, a friend of mine was playing football in the First Division and was soaking up the credit for his success. Then, some weeks later, he was dropped from the team.

Instead of admitting that he was dropped because he was playing badly, he claimed that the manager was no good at picking the team and that he had made the wrong decision. Yet, it was not the manager who had changed but him.

The reason why most people do not devise and run their own improvement programmes is because they have not been honest with themselves about the reasons for their bad results. They blame someone else in order to justify why things did not work out in the way they wanted. They disguise their weaknesses by blaming others for the circumstances in which they find themselves and allow the failures of the past to affect their future.

'we cannot change the past. We can only treat it as a learning curve, a point from which to go forward'

However, we cannot change the past. We can only treat it as a learning curve, a point from which to go forward.

Once we learn to take the credit or blame for whatever has happened, regardless of the consequences, we realise that we can change both ourselves and our future.

It is only when we are honest enough to accept that we create our own worlds and are not just victims of circumstance that we will be on the way to creating that brighter future.

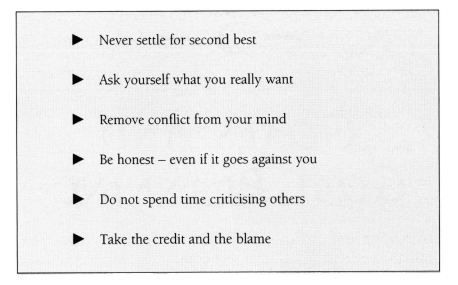

KEY POINTS TO PERFECT VISION

- ▶ Never settle for second best

- ▶ Ask yourself what you really want

- ▶ Remove conflict from your mind

- ▶ Be honest – even if it goes against you

- ▶ Do not spend time criticising others

- ▶ Take the credit and the blame

STEVE DAVIS

"*After trying something, whether you've succeeded or failed, after analysing it honestly, telling yourself that you had no excuses, that you gave it your best shot and there wasn't another thing you could have done to do it any better, then you are a successful person. But, if at the end of it, you ask yourself the question, 'Could I have done it a different and better way?', and in the back of your mind a little person says, 'Yes', then you haven't been successful to yourself.*

Somewhere down the line you may be a more successful person if you actually acknowledge the fact that you're not doing something you enjoy – to change your life, to change your direction. As long as you can ask yourself the questions and come up with the reasons why you're not enjoying it, you're owning up, you're understanding yourself."

ALLISON FISHER

"*I've never achieved enough. I've never reached my capacity, what I think that I'm capable of. I've won four world titles now but it doesn't mean enough to me. I've got more potential. I'm trying to strive for that.*"

59

– 5 –

GOALS AND
GOAL PLANNING

A prerequisite for any improvement programme is for the user to know what he wants to improve in his life. Our thinking needs a focus. It needs a point to work towards. It needs a goal.

The quality of our life is very important to us all, but there are still many of us who wish to improve it without having the goals to do so. We can drift through life without achieving anything and, indeed, without even knowing what we can or should want to achieve. Yet, if we do not plan goals, we are like ships without rudders – we lack direction.

We do not just benefit from having had goals when we achieve them; we gain from the sense of purpose that having a goal gives us; we profit from the lessons we learn on the way. When someone wins the football pools, inherits a large sum of money, or even receives a 'good' divorce settlement, they have money. Yet, monetary reward is actually secondary to the personal satisfaction provided through attaining our goals. When we achieve our goals, we not only receive financial wealth and all it can buy, but we earn the respect and recognition of others as well as ourselves; we add value to ourselves as human beings.

WHAT IS A GOAL?

Most people have dreams. We fantasise about what we would like to be or what we would like to achieve. We say, 'I wouldn't mind a new car' or 'I have half a mind to buy a new dress'; but I do not see these aspirations as goals, I see them as wishes. To my mind, a goal is something you genuinely desire which spurs you into immediate action towards its achievement; it provides an absolutely clear image on which you can focus and which inspires you to get out of bed in the morning.

'a goal is something you genuinely desire which spurs you into immediate action'

A wish can come true without changing your life; but you achieve your goals and, through achieving them, you change the person you are and the person you want to be.

Having a goal is a two-way process. Not only is it the target you aim at; it is the inspiration for its own achievement. It will take you from being merely interested in something to being very committed; and it will be your commitment, your burning desire, that will ensure its attainment. Conversely, the more vague the image in your mind, the more difficult its achievement.

I am sure that we have all been into a little boy's bedroom and seen pictures of cars like Ferraris, Porsches and Maseratis on the wall. Very often, as the boy grows older so the cars are replaced by pictures of attractive ladies in varying states of dress.

Then, when he is 30-35 years old, you see him again. This time he is driving a battered old car and his wife bears little resemblance to the women who had graced his bedroom wall years earlier. So what happened?

'you only have one life so never settle for second best'

Too often we sell our dreams for security. We slip into accepting second best because we are conditioned to believe that we cannot realise the dreams which we had as children.

Yet, had the man kept his dreams and desires he would never have needed to compromise. Had he made his dreams into real goals, he could have achieved them.

Unfortunately, far too frequently we sell ourselves short. Remember, you only have one life so never settle for second best.

ONE GOAL OR MANY?

'the important thing is for you to be absolutely committed to each goal'

You do not have to have one goal, you can have many. You can, if you like, have goals within goals; more immediate aims that act as stepping-stones to the final desired result, in the same way that you might want to travel to Barbados but want to stop off in New York and Miami on the way. You can have goals in different areas of your life, whether at work or at home. The important thing is for you to be absolutely committed to each goal; if you have too many conflicting goals, this will be impossible.

WE ALL NEED GOALS

Have you ever noticed how some people at retirement age are active, lively and still growing as individuals, while others complain, become cynical and do not live a very happy life?

You will have found that the former continue to develop as individuals and still have goals, while the latter merely drift from day to day in an aimless existence.

As children, we all instinctively have goals. We have to learn to walk, to talk, to dress ourselves. As we get older, however, the number of these instinctive goals diminishes. Indeed, instead of acting from instinct or through parental direction, we now have to make our own decisions. Having been previously shaped by outside forces, now we have the free will to shape ourselves. It is now that we desperately need to have goals.

Irrespective of age, if you ever find yourself in a rut, becoming cynical and drifting from day to day, then one of the best medicines you can possibly take is to go back and redefine your goals; give yourself a new target and aim in life.

'give yourself a new target and aim in life'

While you still have goals to achieve you will retain purpose in life. This will stop you from dying as a creative individual who then merely exists until you are buried many years later. Without goals we do not grow, we just get older.

Just imagine what it would be like to be playing a football match with no goal posts and no time on the clock. There would be 22 players out there kicking a ball with no common aim and no definite purpose. That is indeed what real life is like without goals.

'clearly-defined goals keep you motivated and positive'

Without positive goals, people react negatively. When they cease to move forward, when they lack a definite purpose, they become destructive. They focus on the negative things in life and affect not only themselves but the people around them. When you find people walking around criticising others and getting involved in gossip, it is a clear indication that they have ill-defined goals.

Clearly-defined goals keep you motivated and positive, you will live life on purpose and will find that every day will be full of excitement, enthusiasm and creativity. Focusing on your goals will help you to face disappointments and hardships and provide you with the energy and confidence to overcome any obstacle.

So remember, if you are not going forward and developing, if you are not working towards the achievement of a definite goal, then you are actually going backwards. You cannot stand still in life.

GOAL PLANNING

How do we decide exactly what we want from life? Everyone wants something, even the most negative person can start answering the question by deciding what he does not want.

'people who fail to commit their goals to paper rarely achieve them'

Actually, asking yourself the necessary questions for establishing a goal is much easier than it sounds, providing you have an open mind and do not allow your habitual thoughts and behaviour to place restrictions upon you.

Once we have established what we would like to achieve, the next step is to write down our goals. I cannot overstress how important this is. People who fail to commit their goals to paper rarely achieve them.

Some time ago, I was giving a talk on goal planning to one of our sales offices. After telling everyone about the importance of having goals and writing them down, I suddenly realised that I had been telling myself for the past two years that I was going to buy a holiday home on the coast. Yet, because I had failed to write my goal down, I had made no plan or programme for achieving it.

When I left the office that day, I added buying the flat as a priority to my goal list and set a date for the completion of the purchase. I realised that, as I was in the area, the best action I could take was to contact the local estate agents immediately and that evening I viewed some properties. One month from the day I wrote down my goal, we exchanged contracts.

By writing down your goals, you firmly establish them in your mind and make a definite commitment towards their achievement. By committing them to paper, you help maintain your focus and ensure that you take the necessary action to achieve them. Always remember that professionals have to be reminded, not taught; having a written goal is the necessary reminder.

'professionals have to be reminded, not taught'

It is no good, however, if you just write down, 'I want to be a good runner' or 'I want to be a millionaire'. These are just wishes and will not give your subconscious a clearly defined message. You have to give it a clear image on which to focus. If you want to be rich you have to define how much 'rich' is. You would not be able to get a loan from a bank manager if you could not tell him how much you wanted. If what you are saying is that you want to be a millionaire in five years' time, then write that down. Then you can work out exactly what you are going to have to do to achieve it.

As I said before, having a goal is a two-way process: if you have a clear image of what you want, you can plan your programme for achieving the goal by taking mental steps back from the goal as well as towards it. By doing this it will help you to consider all the possible side-effects of your proposed actions and ensure that you express your goals in positive terms.

'keep focusing back and checking that your goal is still a burning desire'

If, for example, you want to lose ten pounds in weight what you must do is state that you are going to lose ten pounds and then punch in the positives to encourage you. Tell yourself that you will be healthier, look slimmer, be able to wear different clothes and it will help you to stick to the programme which will ensure the successful achievement.

Once you have set a goal, however, do not be afraid to change it if you suddenly decide that it is not what you really want. At each stage towards its fulfilment, keep focusing back and checking that your goal is still a burning desire. If it is not, change it. If it is, keep working towards it until you attain the result you required.

'what your mind can conceive and believe in, it can achieve'

Do not concern yourself too much that you will write down impossible goals. In the main, we think on too small a scale and, by now, we should be able to realise that we are capable of achieving a great deal more. Always remember that what your mind can conceive and believe in, it can achieve.

PLAN AND SUPPORT

'the best way to predict the future is to visualise what you want it to be and then go out and create it'

I am often asked, 'How do you see the future?' I answer that the best way to predict the future is to visualise what you want it to be and then go out and create it. But, I stress again, you must consider all the consequences of your creation.

When deciding on your goals, be sure to ask yourself, 'What will be the consequences of my actions?' You will not be a very 'switched on' person and will not develop and grow as an individual if your personal goals end up damaging other people. Make sure, if your goals involve others, that everyone will benefit from your plans.

It might be that, in order to obtain your goals, you would have to work longer hours, neglect your family and eventually risk losing them. When you consider that the reason for working the long hours should be to earn more money for your family, you will realise that the consequences of your actions will far outweigh the end result.

Be sure to assess all the possible outcomes, including the negative ones, that may go along with any of your aims. If there is any conflict, then see if there is a way you can achieve the desired result without the disappointments.

'step out from the crowd and become an individual'

Remember, if your personal goals damage others, you may end up achieving only part of the goal at a cost that will outweigh the benefits and which will prevent you from becoming the type of person you would like to be.

To be successful and reach your goals, you will have to step out from the crowd and become an individual. Yet, once progress begins to set you apart, you will receive criticism from those who have not set their own goals and thus have not been successful. So, when discussing your goals, be careful only to share them with goal-orientated people or individuals who are in the position in which you would like to be.

'only you can stop you permanently'

There will always be those who will tell you, 'It can't be done'. Do not listen to them. Anything is possible if someone has been there before you.

Should any individual start to make you feel negative, or slow you up, remember that they can only stop you temporarily. Only you can stop you permanently.

SET PRIORITIES AND SET A DEADLINE

Once you set down your goals on paper, become totally committed to attaining them. Do not just hope that you will succeed or your goals will become wishes. Place them in order of priority and set a time limit and a timetable for their completion.

It may be that, in order to keep to that timescale, you will have to work harder or be more disciplined with yourself. Unless you write down a completion date for each goal, you will lack the drive that comes from having a deadline; and people without targets have nothing to hit.

'people without targets have nothing to hit'

WHICH SYSTEM OF GOALS IS YOURS?

Before moving on to the next chapter, I would suggest that you consider the categories of goals listed below and ask yourself which you fall into.

NO GOALS	
GOALS, BUT NOT REAL ie. Wishes	
GOALS, BUT NOT WRITTEN DOWN	
WRITTEN GOALS WITHOUT A PLAN FOR ACHIEVEMENT	
WRITTEN GOALS WITH A WRITTEN PLAN	

By clearly defining your type of goals, you can accurately decide on a course of action for their attainment. If you still fall within the first three categories then I would suggest that you consider this chapter further before moving on to the next.

A SIMPLE FORMULA FOR ACHIEVING YOUR GOALS

The information we have discussed in this chapter breaks down into a formula that is easy to remember:

1. Honestly analyse what it is you want.

2. List your goals on paper.

3. Place the listed goals in their order of priority.

4. Allocate a completion date to each.

5. Keep reviewing your goals to ensure that they are sufficiently important to you.

6. Plan the action needed to obtain your goals.

Goal Planning works both for major goals and for the things which, for one reason or another, we have been meaning to do but have not actually achieved yet. It could be taking your spouse out for a meal or to the theatre, going to Paris for the weekend, taking your daughter ice-skating, or even taking your dog for a walk in a special park.

By working the formula – committing your goals to paper, allocating a completion date, writing down your plan for the goal's attainment, acting upon it and crossing it from your list – you will start achieving things which you never have before. This will get you into the habit of goal achieving and enable you to move on to your larger goals.

'you will rarely find a goal achiever who is good in only one area'

It is for this reason that you will rarely find a goal achiever who is good in only one area. Once they have found the formula to achieve, and have the proof of its success, then they use it in all areas of their lives.

Remember, if your goals are important enough, you will definitely make them happen. By defining, planning and scheduling their achievement you have taken a major step on your path to success.

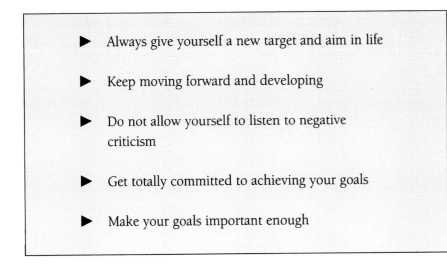

- ▶ Always give yourself a new target and aim in life

- ▶ Keep moving forward and developing

- ▶ Do not allow yourself to listen to negative criticism

- ▶ Get totally committed to achieving your goals

- ▶ Make your goals important enough

ROBERT SWAN

I was, and am, still no different than anyone. I was 18 years of age when I said, 'I'm going to walk to the South Pole', and exactly ten years later I had turned that dream into reality.

People ask me whether individuals can make a difference to their own lives, well, sure they can! Basically, if they plan things, prepare themselves right and go for it, anything is possible.

PETER ELLIOTT

You have always got to have something to aim for otherwise you just keep going through the motions. It is best to have a goal to reach for. My aim is to be Olympic Champion. The pinnacle of my career will be the Olympic games and, hopefully, winning it. Obviously, I am striving to win other races before then, but this is my long-term ambition.

– 6 –

MAKING
THE CHANGE

*'if we want our
lives and
ourselves to
improve we must
be prepared to
change'*

Now that we have our goals clearly defined we have to begin making the changes which will enable us to achieve them.

To do this, we have to recognise that things do not change; it is we ourselves and our attitude towards whatever situations we face which will need to alter, if we are to grow and progress. It is within our own world that any changes must occur before we can benefit from any change in our external world.

If we want our lives and ourselves to improve then, first of all, we must be prepared to change.

One of the real keys to success is for us to strive actively for constructive change. The tendency for all of us is to resist change because we are conditioned to believe that it will normally be 'for the worse'.

Change usually involves new and unfamiliar feelings, which can initially be unsettling. For many of us it is easier to remain safe, secure and living in the manner to which we are accustomed rather than to risk a little discomfort.

Yet, becoming uncomfortable and experiencing new situations and feelings is a sure sign that we are growing and improving. Once we understand the difference that an alteration in our attitude, our appearance and our approach can make, we will become less hesitant about making those changes. If we refuse to accept change we will always get what we always have – similar results as in the past.

The main thing to remember is that changes will not happen overnight but that, providing we give them time, we will eventually reap the rewards we seek. The very first step needed for change is to really desire it. We rarely take the necessary steps to change unless we really want to.

THE HABITS OF A LIFETIME

When we talk about making the change, what we are really talking about is changing the habits of a lifetime. We already know from the chapter on thinking that our thoughts are the very first thing which we must alter if we are to improve.

Just to stress the importance of getting your thinking right you might want to consider the book entitled *Think, And Grow Rich* by Napoleon Hill. I often say that people get as far as 'Think', but they do not ever grow rich. It is also worth noting that the book was not called, 'Grow Rich and Think'. The obvious point is that the very first change we must make is in our thinking.

Our next step must be to look at each section of our lives and assess what it is that we need to change in order to move nearer to becoming the person we really want to be.

We are all aware of things about ourselves which we would like to change, or of the changes which we know we must

'becoming uncomfortable and experiencing new situations and feelings is a sure sign that we are growing and improving'

make in order to progress. But it is one thing to know something and quite another to act on that knowledge.

'if you change today you will see a reward for your efforts that much sooner'

Very often we make ourselves wait for changes: we promise to change in the New Year or when we start a new job. But New Year's resolutions seldom last and, as we have already said, the benefits of any changes do not happen overnight. If you change today you will see a reward for your efforts that much sooner, you will have taken another step along that road to the improved you. So make the change now.

Once we have changed our thinking, we have an opportunity to create new and better habits which will help us towards the success we so strongly desire. Day by day, hour by hour, we must concentrate on the type of person we want to be. Then, we must decide on the actions we must take to achieve success and then make a habit of them.

A CHANGE FOR GOOD

'do not ever underestimate the power of consistency, it has a compounding effect.'

I always notice on the courses and lectures I run the positive change of attitude of the delegates. They leave the meetings as high as a balloon: new people with strong desires who believe they can rule the world.

Then, two or three weeks later, I will go to a meeting and talk to the same individuals who remind me of little soggy deflated balloons and I wonder what has happened to them. When they left my meeting they were on the ceiling and now they are on the floor.

The reason is that, in spite of what happens today, most people will continue to do tomorrow what they did yesterday. Any changes we make must not be temporary; we must work consistently to ensure that they are permanent. Do not ever underestimate the power of consistency, it has a compounding effect.

Have you ever heard the saying, 'Money makes money and the money money makes makes more money'?

I often pose the question to people that if I were to give them £1.00 and their money doubled every day, how long would it take for them to become millionaires? The answers I have had range from five to fifteen years.

The answer is actually 21 days. On the first day you have one pound, by the second it is two, by the third it is four, by the fourth it is eight, and so on, until you reach over one million pounds on the twenty-first day.

You can see the effect of compound interest. However, it will only be effective provided you give it time to take effect. The longer you allow something to compound, whether it be good or bad, the greater the effect.

'the longer you allow something to compound, whether it be good or bad, the greater the effect'

So, let us see how this could possibly go wrong. Just imagine that I had promised you that you would make £1 million in 21 days by following my scheme and that by the seventh day you only had £64 – a far cry from the promised million. Your belief could falter and you could well start to question the validity of my claim. You might then take the worst option and ask the opinion of someone who did not know the system. If their advice led you to stop, even for just one day, you would not reach the £1 million on the twenty-first day as promised. At that stage you would probably declare that the system did not work. The fact of the matter is that no system can work if you do not follow it.

'we have to follow through until we have achieved the required results'

Indeed, with any change, we have to follow through until we have achieved the required results.

TO BE, TO DO, TO HAVE

Whenever I ask individuals about what they would like from life the answer usually relates to what they would like to have – 'I'd like to have a better figure', 'a bigger house' or 'a new car'.

'firstly people see you, then they hear you, so it is essential to promote ourselves in a positive manner'

But, in order to 'have' something there are two other stages which we must first go through. In order to 'have' we have to 'do' – that is take the actions to achieve it. And in order to 'do' we have to 'be' the person who can achieve it.

We already know that in order to 'be' we have to change. We have tackled our thinking and now believe that change is possible. The next step is to break it down further and concentrate on each of the individual areas of our lives that we feel requires improvement, remembering that our major aim is to obtain much better results. After all, I am sure that none of us would be too happy if, after investing so much time and effort in changing, we ended up achieving the same results as before.

CHANGING OUR APPEARANCE

A good place to start the change is in our appearance. Firstly people see you, then they hear you, so it is essential that we take this opportunity to promote ourselves in a positive manner.

About three years ago, when I was due to have an Anterior Cruciate ligament operation on my knee, I wanted to make sure that I was making the right decision, so I visited the surgeon to ask his advice.

He looked just as I had always imagined a surgeon would look – his confidence in what he was saying, his general manner and his appearance all contributed to my belief that he was highly capable in his field. I did not see any evidence of his ability – until after the operation – nor did I ask for his qualifications. I believed in him simply because he looked and acted the part.

Now just imagine what my reaction would have been had he been wearing plimsolls, had holes in his jeans, an earring in one ear and had had one too many scotches. He would have had to have been an excellent salesman to have convinced me to go ahead with the operation.

Whatever you want to become, be it a surgeon, lawyer, salesman, professional footballer or even a popstar, you must first dress to look the part.

People form immediate impressions and the very first person to form an impression will be you. So to get where we want to go in life we have to begin by dressing as though we are already there. Our dress reflects our overall mood, so that when we dress well we feel good and have confidence in ourselves and when we have confidence, we inspire it in others.

Similarly when people have cosmetic surgery they feel much happier and grow in confidence. It is almost as though the operation has been performed on their brain.

In my football days I played for a series of clubs and every club had a different strategy. But I found that the better quality clubs obtaining the best results all concentrated on the attitude of the players.

On match days one of the first things we did was to dress in a similar way. By doing so we felt part of something important and it confirmed in our minds that we were in a professional outfit that was going to achieve outstanding results.

'whatever you want to become you must first dress to look the part'

So, in the unlikely event of me ever returning to football as a manager, my perfect vision would be to see my team as the fittest, healthiest and smartest in the league. Once I had created that kind of professionalism in the club I would fully expect outstanding results.

'you do not get a second chance to make a first impression'

If you change your appearance you will change the way you feel about yourself and change people's reactions to you. It is worth remembering that you do not get a second chance to make a first impression.

CHANGING OUR ATTITUDE

We have said in a previous chapter that very often we cannot change the situation, all we can do is change our attitude towards it. For some of us a change in attitude will take a slight adjustment. For others it will need a complete change in the way we think.

'every one of us can make a difference to someone else's life'

We all underestimate the power which, collectively, we hold as individuals. Every one of us can make a difference to someone else's life and what we need to do is to get into the habit of using that power.

Just imagine getting into a lift one morning and saying, 'Hi' to the person with whom you are sharing the space. What will their response be? I imagine that it would be, 'Hi'.

Now imagine the same scenario with you getting into the lift, smiling and saying, 'Hi, good morning, how are you today'. It is unlikely that their answer will be just 'Hi'.

Remember that whatever you give out in life you should get back. So if you give out five words you should get five back and if you give out ten words, you should get back ten. Even if you do not, what do you lose?

Get into the habit of smiling more. It only takes 14 muscles to smile compared with the 72 it takes to frown. It is infectious, easy and almost impossible to be miserable when you have got a smile on your face.

THE ART OF COMPLIMENTS AND COMMUNICATION

Think of the difference it makes to you when someone pays you a compliment and yet think how rarely compliments are given or received.

'think how rarely compliments are given or received'

Now consider what your reaction would be if one of your friends called and the only purpose of the call was to compliment you. It only goes to show how little we compliment each other.

All too often people are filled with regret at funerals because they had not said what they wanted. So do not wait, start now. It is no use walking behind a friend's coffin and saying what a nice person they were. Tell them while they are alive. My challenge to you today is to ring someone just to tell them how much they mean to you.

Do you know the best time to tell your spouse that you love them? Before someone else does!

By realising what we can create, we begin to realise our potential as human beings. We can change our environment around us as well as ourselves.

All successful people know that it is the little things that make the big difference. By our attitude to other people we not only help them but, in return, they help us to keep positive and happy.

BECOME ENTHUSIASTIC

There is only one thing almost as contagious as enthusiasm: that is the lack of it. There are always times of the year when people are positive and enthusiastic – just think of how we were as children at Christmas. But why wait for a special time of year, or for a particular day?

You will find that the key is to be enthusiastic about everything you do. I have never yet met a successful person who is not full of excitement and does not have a passion for living. When you start getting enthusiastic about life every day is Christmas day.

SUCCESS IS CAUGHT NOT TAUGHT

In Chapter Two, I explained the influence that our environment has on us as we develop our thought processes. As children our only guide to life is our parents and if they are not working to a successful formula then it is unlikely that, initially, we will.

'our minds are like magnets for information'

Because it feeds our minds as we change, we have to continue to be very careful of our environment.

Our minds are like magnets for information. So be sure to only pick up what you want and if what you have picked up is not going to get you to where you want to go then discard it.

If you run across the most negative person in a room why not check with whom they are having lunch. I can almost guarantee that it will be the second most negative person. Any chance they might have for success slowly slips away as they feed each other negative thoughts during their time together.

In the main, you will find that people go around with those

who are like-minded and getting similar results. Yet, by mixing with individuals of a similar level as yourself you will just stay at your current level.

The best way to improve is to become exceedingly uncomfortable through mixing with people who have achieved outstanding results in whatever field you wish to conquer.

You will normally find that successful people are willing to share that success and experience with others. In the unlikely

event, however, that you meet an achiever who has become 'self-important' – a legend in his own lunch-time – just consider what his 'achievement' means in personal terms. I should also say that he might be exactly the type of person who throws away his success through complacency. I am certain that you would not want to become an individual like that so would not want to model yourself on him anyway.

'success is caught, not taught. Get uncomfortable. Mix with winners'

Always ask yourself, are the people with whom I am spending my time getting me closer to, or further away from, my goals? Success is caught not taught and your environment is very, very important. So get uncomfortable. Mix with winners.

Remember the saying, 'If you want to fly with the eagles, don't scratch around in the barnyard with the turkeys'.

HOW TO MAKE THE CHANGES

Always remember that, if you can find an important enough reason to change, you will certainly find out what actions to take – if you can find out why, you will find out how.

'if you can find out why, you will find out how'

There is, however, a formula to enable you to make the changes which we have discussed:

1. Focus on the changes you need. Visualise each change as if it has already happened. Concentrate on the pleasure you will experience after the change and acknowledge the pain of not changing.

2. Find a true leader to follow; not just a talker but someone who has achieved the results you desire and commands your respect.

3. Have a monitor to enable you to keep checking on your progress.

4. If you are not on the right route change your direction, not your decision to go.

In a matter of time you will either be very pleased that you made these changes or very sad that you did not.

Cultivate your own Perfect Vision to create a fantastic new future by changing the habits which have held you back in the past.

'you will either be very pleased that you made these changes or very sad that you did not'

KEY POINTS TO PERFECT VISION

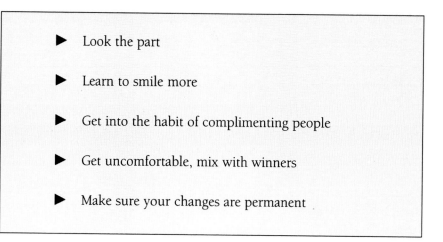

> ▶ Look the part
>
> ▶ Learn to smile more
>
> ▶ Get into the habit of complimenting people
>
> ▶ Get uncomfortable, mix with winners
>
> ▶ Make sure your changes are permanent

IAN BOTHAM

"*Once you start doing something solely as a job, you lose the interest, flair and excitement that the game gives you. To me, the game of cricket excites me. I get up every morning and I do not know what is going to happen that day – I could get 100 or 0 – but I know that if I go out there and give it every shot anything could happen. Enjoy the game you are playing, want to play and, if you want to play, you will do well.*"

ROBERT SWAN

"*There can't be any limits. You just come up to an obstacle and say 'right, how do I overcome this problem?' We either go through it or go around it but, in my language, you don't just stop and think about it and talk about it, you do something about the problem.*

Nothing is easy if you want a challenge. That is why it is called a challenge. But the way that I do things is to never take 'no' for an answer. There is always a way through – ask people, communicate with people – and you'll get through. 'No' doesn't exist in my language."

JOHN BARNES

"*No matter how good you are, you will never know that you are the best until you put yourself with the best and see that you are coping with it; that you are either better than, or as good as, them.*"

– 7 –

HEALTHY BODY

One thing that people always ask me is, 'How would you feel, if you lost all of your wealth?' My answer is that, so long as you left me with my health and my attitude, it would be a very short while until I got it all back.

I have spent many hours developing individuals on the road to success and I always ask the question, 'Are you looking to become a millionaire?' When they say 'yes', I then ask them, 'Assuming someone was involved in a car crash, lost the sight of one eye and was given £1 million compensation would you change places with them? Similarly, if they had lost an arm or a leg and received £1 million compensation would you swap places?'

The answer in every case is 'no', because whatever you earn or obtain in life is dependent on enjoying good health.

I am sure that the majority of us have never thought about what a wonderful and complex machine the body is. For instance, did you know that if your arteries, capillaries and veins were joined end to end they would stretch almost 60,000 miles? Or that your heart pumps a cupful of blood with every

'whatever you earn or obtain in life is dependent on enjoying good health'

'I am sure that the majority of us have never thought about what a wonderful and complex machine the body is'

beat and that it pumps nine pints of blood around a complete circuit of your system approximately every minute?

Our bodies are actually designed to carry us through 120 years of life, but we destroy ourselves with the likes of worry, stress, smoking and alcohol, all of which contribute to slowing us down and, in some cases, stopping us altogether.

LOOKING AFTER THE MACHINE

'how do you view your body?'

Let me ask you, 'How do you view your body?' Is it totally overweight and just something which is going to take you from birth to death or is it something that you are going to develop and build to ensure that it takes you from A to B in the best possible way?

Your body should be important to you – it is the only one you have and it is going to take you from the beginning of your life to the end. If you had only one car, you would obviously

not put vinegar in the engine. You would put in oil because that is the right ingredient. Yet, a considerable number of people take better care of their cars than they do of themselves.

Just imagine that you had a brand new racing car and you wanted to win a Grand Prix. You would not put mud in the carburettor and still expect it to win the race. Yet that is exactly what we do with our bodies. What we have to realise, if we are sluggish and performing badly, is that we are putting the wrong fuel in our engines.

'look after the body as well as the brain'

What we have to do is work out what we are taking into our bodies to ensure that the fuel we are providing will give us the best results. If we want to perform properly then there are enough books on diets and food intake to advise us, but we have to re-learn our eating habits. Change the fuel and you will improve the performance.

HIGH ENERGY

You are going to need a tremendous amount of physical energy to fulfil your potential and I would thoroughly recommend regularly working out. Get totally fit and look after the body as well as the brain.

'a fit average person will always have the edge on an unfit talented person'

You will then have plenty of energy to make the most use of the talents you have. A fit average person will always have the edge on an unfit talented person, so we must concentrate on keeping fit while working towards our goals.

If we look after our health we will not only live longer, but feel better. When we feel good about ourselves and have our bodies toned up our self-image is much higher and we have more self-respect.

NO ARTIFICIAL STIMULUS

Successful, positive people do not require artificial stimulus. Their enthusiasm and excitement for life is the only stimulus they need.

We are all living in a stressful world and the greater our achievements the greater the pressures placed upon us. Because of this, if we drink to relax, or smoke to keep calm, then the greater the pressure we face, the greater is our reliance on our own particular antidote. What started out as the occasional drink, or occasional cigarette, becomes more frequent until it becomes a habit that is hard to break.

'a healthy positive person can overcome any stress, strain or pressure'

This programme can only lead you into an unhealthy condition. A healthy positive person can overcome any stress, strain or pressure. They do not need to rely on artificial stimulus.

DO NOT ABUSE YOUR HEALTH

I am sure that, now you have understood the concept of Perfect Vision, you will appreciate the need for many people to make a change in their attitudes towards alcohol and cigarettes. Statistics confirm that making this kind of change is particularly difficult

No one is suggesting that people smoke in order to try and give themselves cancer or get drunk so they can become alcoholics. People over-indulge through habit; a habit or habits they originally formed because they followed a leader, or thought when they started that they were being 'adult', or again because they believed that they were relieving pressure and aiding their socialising.

If you smoke, focus on the potential damage you may do to yourself and learn to hate cigarettes. If you drink to excess, focus on the difficulties caused by it and learn to moderate your drinking. Understand what you are creating and take immediate action to change.

Have a little discomfort now to avoid a lot of pain later.

ALCOHOL

'visualise the outcome if you continue with your existing habits'

I cannot tell you how many times I have walked into a hotel breakfast room to see people whose eyes are all bloodshot and who look like they have been run over. When you ask them what happened they come up with the phrase, 'I had a good night last night'. I am not sure what they would look like after a bad one!

Try considering the effects of drinking excessive amounts of alcohol, in terms of accidents, the crime rate, your heart and your liver.

Whilst I am not advocating that everyone become teetotal, I know that many individuals would benefit from restricting their intake of alcohol, especially as it is attributed to being the possible cause of 40,000 deaths a year.

'you cannot be the best you can possibly be if you mess up your system'

It is obvious that you cannot be the best you can possibly be if you mess up your system. How would you feel if a surgeon who has just had a few drinks was to operate on you or a pilot in the same condition was about to fly you home?

CIGARETTES

I am sure that you can make a decision based on facts, so let us have a look at some. Listed below are the figures, released by the Medical Statistics Unit, for potentially smoking-related deaths, in England and Wales, for 1989:

MAIN DIAGNOSIS

Malignant neoplasm: Trachea, bronchus and lung	34,581
Lip, oral cavity and pharynx	1,716
Oesophagus	5,008
Larynx	861
Diseases of the Circulatory System	
Ischaemic heart disease	150,794
Chronic pulmonary heart disease	649
Aortic aneurysm	8,251
Diseases of the Respiratory System	
Bronchitis and emphysema	8,680
Chronic airways obstruction (not elsewhere classified)	18,948

(Source: Medical Statistics Unit)

One can set alongside these statistics showing potentially-related deaths further figures that specifically link 301 deaths per day to smoking. Now, let me put that into perspective. I am sure that we all remember the tragic incident in December 1988 when the Pan Am aircraft exploded in mid-air over Lockerbie with the loss of everyone on board and 11 on the ground. Well, the number of smoking-related deaths is equivalent to eight Lockerbie disasters each week – and yet smoking is still something which people do voluntarily!

It fascinated me that, for a few months after the Lockerbie incident, people were uneasy about flying and yet they had no hesitation in continuing to smoke.

With all the facts and knowledge available, it always amazes me when someone is a genuine friend and you see another individual offer them a cigarette. They say, 'Here, have one of mine' and your friend says, 'Thank you very much'.

'the number of smoking-related deaths is equivalent to eight Lockerbie disasters each week'

If you have a friend who smokes, have a bit of vision. They are definitely ruining their health so try to get them to break their habit before their habit breaks them. And I do mean break the habit, not just cut down.

Some weeks ago I was speaking to a group of managers. One of them had attended a previous course where she had been persuaded to give up smoking, but she had later gone back to the habit. She approached me to say that she was pleased because she had finally managed to cut down again to just two a day.

What she did not realise was that she was actually telling me that she was still going in the wrong direction, only more slowly.

If you are doing something which is damaging your health, slowing down may mean that you might live a little bit longer but it will not stop you doing damage to yourself.

'if you are going in the wrong direction, turn around and go back the way you have just come'

If you are going in the wrong direction, for example, if you are heading south instead of north, you do not just need to slow down but to turn around and go back the way you have just come.

If you are in any doubt about whether you are going the wrong way then ask yourself a couple of simple questions. What are the benefits of smoking? I would suggest that there are none. It makes you smell, costs you money and stains your teeth and fingers. Now ask yourself honestly whether you feel that there might be even more damaging consequences. With cigarettes the answer can only be 'yes'.

So take heavy action now. Stop immediately. Make a decision and stick with it. If you were taken into hospital and told that you had only seven days to live unless you gave up smoking you would give up immediately. Do not wait until it becomes a necessity. Have a little vision and take positive action now.

'if nothing else in this book influences you, try to give up the smoking habit before you become a statistic'

If nothing else in this book influences you, try to give up the smoking habit before you become a statistic.

Once you have changed your habit, you will benefit twice over. Firstly, to realise that you control your habits and not vice versa and you will feel better about yourself.

Secondly, you will see other people who still smoke and you will know that you have done something that they have yet to achieve. It will spur you on to greater action in other things because you will know that you are an achiever.

THE SNOWBALL EFFECT

When it comes down to something as important as your health I do suggest that you act immediately. There are many things which are not good for our health – excessive alcohol, cigarettes, drug abuse – all of these are ingredients for disaster and can stop you from getting to where you want to go.

But we do not become chain smokers, alcoholics or drug addicts overnight. Addiction is a result of what I call the snowball effect.

Ask yourself, 'From where does an alcoholic or drug addict start?' We all know where they ultimately finish. If you see a drunk in the middle of a high street you should realise that he did not become like that overnight. It took a period of time.

At one time he probably used to have an occasional drink, but then along came situations with which he could not cope and he started to try to drink his way out of them. In actual fact, he drank himself right to where he is now: homeless and drinking all day long until he kills himself.

Habits are like snowballs going down the hill. Whether it is a good or bad habit it will gather momentum and size. So, the sooner we take our habits in hand and make them work for us, as opposed to against us, the better.

I am sure that now you are developing your Perfect Vision, you will change your whole approach to your body. Remember that you are the only person that you will neither leave nor lose. Your body is without doubt the most wonderful gift you have ever received. Treasure it.

'whether it is a good or bad habit it will gather momentum and size'

KEY POINTS TO PERFECT VISION

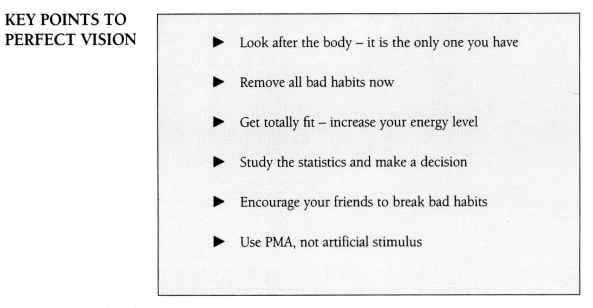

▶ Look after the body – it is the only one you have

▶ Remove all bad habits now

▶ Get totally fit – increase your energy level

▶ Study the statistics and make a decision

▶ Encourage your friends to break bad habits

▶ Use PMA, not artificial stimulus

ALLISON FISHER

"It's healthy body, healthy mind. I think that's part of the thing that separates certain people. To be healthy is very important. I see it as a way of releasing tension. I found that when I was playing squash, a year to six months ago, it did me good in snooker. I was very positive and didn't want to give up."

PETER ELLIOTT

"Health is very important and I do not think that people appreciate just how important it is. I am not saying that I am a health freak, but I do watch what I eat. I can appreciate how it feels to be very fit and when I retire I shall still carry on doing some form of exercise because I would never want to feel unfit. A healthy diet and way of life is very important."

STEVE DAVIS

"If you don't look after yourself you really are lowering your chances. I think if you want to last longer you've got to do that. It is well known that the fitter you are, the more mentally alert you are."

– 8 –

ACT

I have helped to develop people in the past who have got their visualisation, thinking and believing working for them; they have been honest with themselves about what they want out of life; and they have established their goals. Yet, even then, they have not achieved their desired result.

This is because they failed to act. The difference between achievers and non-achievers is not just knowledge, it is action. We do not get rewarded for what we know; we get rewarded for what we do.

I often sit with individuals who want to create a new life for themselves, who have all the knowledge about what is needed, but who still fail to act. They tell me, 'I know that' and I reply, 'I know you know it but you don't do it'.

The key to making the change necessary for the 'new you' is for you, yourself, to create and run a programme for attaining your goals.

Consciously or subconsciously, we all use programmes for different aspects of life. Think of the airline pilot who is

'the difference between achievers and non-achievers is not just knowledge, it is action'

returning you from your holiday into London Heathrow airport. His goal is to arrive at Heathrow, but to achieve this he obviously has to run a programme.

'do not ever underestimate the power of programming'

The flight plan has to be worked out so that he takes the most direct route, he has to calculate the estimated time of arrival, the amount of fuel he will require and the flying height. He will continually monitor and check his programme to make sure that he is on course as the flight continues and will make any adjustments should he be blown off course by the wind.

The pilot may change his direction but never his decision to go.

Similarly we must always keep our goal in mind and work a programme for its achievement, adjusting our actions when necessary to overcome any situation or obstacle which could take us further away from our goals.

Do not ever underestimate the power of programming. All you need to do is follow the written programme and then it is not a case of whether you will achieve, but a case of when.

To be successful, we have to run a programme for success. We all run programmes on other things, such as fitness, learning a new sport, etc. We all can have, and do have, Perfect Vision: think of the programmes we run for our holidays. We plan all year round for that two weeks. We choose our destination with care, we book the trip, we take out travel insurance. What we have to do now is to use the same system we use for everyday achievements to ensure we attain our more important goals.

'there is absolutely no limit to any self-improvement programme'

There is absolutely no limit to any self-improvement pro-gramme; the key is to run your programme *until* you are successful. Decide on the actions that will enable you to fulfil whatever you have on your goal list, get a written programme for its achievement and then take consistent action.

WRITTEN PROGRAMMES

Let us assume that you have a burning desire to lose weight and that you have listed this as your top priority, with a completion date of three months' time. Your next step is to work out how much you would have to lose each day to ensure that you meet your target weight by the allocated date.

Then you would need to decide exactly how you could achieve this. It might be through a different diet or more exercise or a combination of both, but whatever you decide upon you need to write it down.

A typical exercise programme might look something like this:

Name	Mon	Tues	Wed	Thurs	Fri	Sat	Sun	Target	Achieved
Running								15 miles	
Press Ups								500	
Sit Ups								500	
Rowing								15,000 metres	
Exercise Bike								20 miles	
Weight Loss								2lb	
Lengths								70	

PROGRAMMES ARE THERE TO BE FOLLOWED. TARGETS ARE THERE TO BE ACHIEVED.

WE WILL ACT *UNTIL* . . . !

The vast majority of people who get this far and do not achieve their goals have not set out the programme to attain them.

'the vast majority of people who get this far and do not achieve their goals have not set out the programme to attain them'

CONSISTENT ACTION

It does not matter how many sheets of paper, with goals and programmes on them, that you have stacked in your drawer, if you do not actually put them into action.

The biggest cause of failure is through not sticking to a programme. We get distracted and blown off course too easily.

To be successful, we need to act consistently. It is no good dieting for three days then reverting back to our previous eating habits. Three-day diets do not work. We have to take consistent action on our chosen programme and continue following it until we achieve the results we require.

'the biggest cause of failure is through not sticking to a programme'

To encourage us to stick to the programme we will need a monitor. In the case of a diet, it would be a set of scales and possibly a tape measure – something that will give us concrete evidence that the programme which we are running is moving us toward our end goal.

We have already said that change takes time; but, providing we continue to adhere to the programme, the results will come in the end.

'three-day diets do not work'

ADJUSTING YOUR PROGRAMME

If, however, after a reasonable amount of time, we do not begin to get the results we require, we must then look at adjusting the programme.

We must consider whether we have been sticking to the programme we originally set, and whether by failing to take consistent action, we are ourselves the cause of our lack of results.

There is obviously no point in adjusting the programme if we have not been keeping to it in the first place.

THE WRONG PROGRAMME

It is easy to identify when the programme is not working. If you have correctly visualised your goal and the action you are taking is not moving you closer to it, then change the programme.

If you turned on the television and it was showing ice-hockey when you wanted to watch football you would obviously have no hesitation in changing the channel to get you back to the right programme.

'money talks and for most people it says, "Goodbye"'

SAVINGS PROGRAMMES

When we use a little vision we can head off potential difficulties. I am sure you have heard the phrase that, 'Money talks', well, for most people it says, "Goodbye".

There are a considerable number of people who throughout their working lives have money troubles; they are either overdrawn at the bank, have a mortgage which they continually struggle to meet, or use credit cards that accrue massive amounts of interest on the debt, and only make things even worse.

Then, at retirement, comes the real sacrifice. They are no longer able to work. They are short of money and so are dependent on the state and/or their friends and relatives.

Statistics point to the conclusion that, of 100 people who started out at the age of 20 years, hopeful, cheerful and planning to be rich, at retirement, one will be wealthy, four will be well-to-do, five will be self-supporting, 36 will be dead and 54 will be dependent on the state, relatives or charity.

There is, however, really no need to be in this situation. It just takes planning and programming to make your money work for you.

We live in a 'buy now, pay later' society which might seem a good idea at the time but certainly does not when 'later' comes. Do you realise that when you do not make adequate provision for your retirement it is not always because you have not earned enough money?

'when we hit a tough time we must not stop, we must keep working the programme because the programme works'

Let us take a look at an individual who started work at 17 years of age and retired at 60. Let us assume that he started on an income of £6,000 per year and his income was increased by 10% per annum. If he only invested 5% of his monies, leaving 95% to cover all other expenses, and on the money he was investing he received 10% interest per annum, he would have accrued a lump sum of £744,160 at the age of 60 – remember the compound effect.

If you are 30 years of age, retire at the age of 60 and are paid monthly that is just 360 pay days until retirement.

The reason that so many people have so little money at retirement is that when a difficult financial time appears – and we all have them – they stop their savings programme. As with our self-improvement programme, when we hit a tough time we must not stop, we must keep working the programme because the programme works.

Always remember that tough times never last but tough people do.

I have found that people at retirement age are either very pleased that they took out a retirement benefit scheme or very sad that they did not. But just in case you are in any doubt just visualise these two different scenarios and see which one you would choose:

1. You could either be short of money and just making ends meet, queuing up at the Post Office every week and being dependent on your friends, relatives and the state.

Or

2. Have more money than you need being credited to your account and continue to watch your fund grow and make more money for you each week.

If, like most people, you would prefer the latter, I would suggest that you take the action now and pay the premium; rather than eventually paying the price for not visualising and running the programme for your future. Start now.

'people at retirement age are either very pleased that they took out a retirement benefit scheme or very sad that they did not'

'there is a programme for success and a programme for failure'

STAYING ON TRACK

There is a programme for success and a programme for failure and we have to have a written programme to keep us consistently on track.

The programme formula for success is as follows:

1. Seek the knowledge and information which will help you decide upon the action to be taken.

2. Allocate a definite time for taking action.

3. Consistently stick to the programme.

4. Have a monitor to ensure you are progressing towards your goal.

5. Adjust the programme if you are not getting the desired results.

Let us have a look at two examples of how this system works.

Paul is aged 28 years and was a non-swimmer. When discussing goal planning he put on his list that he wanted to learn how to swim. The reason that he had not been able to swim for all these years was because he had not made it important enough to become a goal and did not have a programme to achieve this.

Paul's programme was:

1. He sought out the individual who could teach him to swim.

2. He booked up a series of lessons.

3. He set a definite time for his attendance.

4. He attended regularly until he had succeeded in learning.

In Paul's particular case he is so enthusiastic about the sport that he is now going for his life saving certificate and realises that for 28 years he was just running the wrong programme.

'in Paul's particular case he realises that for 28 years he was just running the wrong programme'

Our second example, David, is also 28 years of age, and was two-and-a-half stone overweight. David listed his desired weight and we decided to put into action a three-month programme.

He stuck to the programme for the first month and was, indeed, ahead of his target, but then he eased back and started to increase his intake of food and also began to cut corners on his exercise programme.

David realised that the main reason he was falling behind target was because he was slipping back into his old habits of consuming large amounts of food. So, to help him get back on track, we decided to put little notes inside his fridge and food cupboard to remind him of his programme.

'remind yourself that achievers with vision put things right before they go wrong'

Remember that unusual people do unusual things and achievers do not need to be taught, just reminded. So, if you find yourself flicking back into your old habits, remind yourself that achievers with vision put things right before they go wrong. Non-achievers try to put them right after they have gone wrong.

Both David and Paul achieved their goals by having a written programme and consistently taking action. Remember that people who are very, very serious about their programming get some very serious results.

'a lot of individuals get eaten up in the system because they do not have goals or programmes'

Working a programme will definitely create new and outstanding results so when visualising your achievements always see an oak tree, not an acorn.

Acorns do become oak trees. A lot of acorns are, however, eaten by the squirrels before they have had a chance to become fully-grown trees. Similarly a lot of individuals get eaten up in the system because they do not have goals or programmes to achieve the outstanding results of which they are definitely capable.

Many people think about it, many people dream about it, many people talk about it, but very few people act. It is action that produces the results so make sure that you take heavy consistent action on your improvement programme.

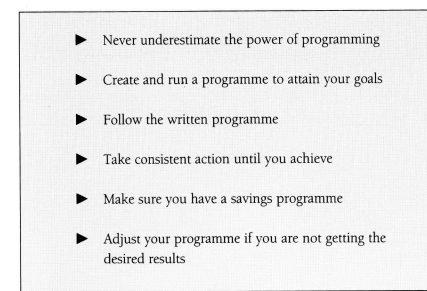

The box contains the following points:

▶ Never underestimate the power of programming

▶ Create and run a programme to attain your goals

▶ Follow the written programme

▶ Take consistent action until you achieve

▶ Make sure you have a savings programme

▶ Adjust your programme if you are not getting the desired results

66 *What motivates me beyond anything is the fact that I have never seen the second hand on my watch going backwards. We are given one chance and my whole ethic is to just go for it. Every single second of your life isn't going to happen again. This is not a dress rehearsal, this is it.* 99

**ROBERT
SWAN**

66 *You will not improve because you want to, you improve because you make it happen. You have got to find the ways to improve, make yourself a promise to improve and then actually carry it out. If you want something important like the improvement in your career or the way you want to do things in your life, then you have actually got to put yourself out.* 99

**STEVE
PERRYMAN**

66 *No one is going to hand you anything on a plate and so you have to work hard, be dedicated and persistent in aiming for your goals. I always say that, if you do not taste the disappointments in life you will never appreciate the successes. Persevere at what you are doing and do not be side-tracked by other people. At the end of the day, if you work hard and are dedicated, then you will pull through.* 99

**PETER
ELLIOTT**

– 9 –

VITAL INGREDIENTS FOR SUCCESS

'the key to success is to keep working your programme until you have completed the task'

W e have reached the stage of Perfect Vision where we recognise that all of the separate components of our improvement system must come together to ensure we achieve our goals.

An improvement programme, however, can obviously never work if it is never started. It has no chance, either, unless it is followed properly and consistently.

I cannot stress enough, at this stage, the importance of following the entire programme. You will not achieve the results you desire if you are only prepared to adopt those parts of the programme you find comfortable and ignore the parts which you find more difficult.

So follow through. The key to success is to keep working your programme until you have completed the task. Individuals who achieve the greatest success are those who have worked their programmes *until* they have achieved their aims.

That is not to say that they succeeded the first time, but that their goals were important enough for them to learn from their experience, adjust their programmes and continue. They did not get disheartened and give up, but persisted in the pursuit of their goals until they achieved the results they sought.

*　　*　　*　　*　　*

There are a number of crucial ingredients to help in your pursuit of excellence, when working your programme.

TRY, FAIL AND ADJUST

It would be a rarity, in any improvement programme, to get things right the first time. We have to be prepared both repeatedly to fail and to learn from those failures, continually adjusting our programme to ensure that we stay on track.

'we have to be prepared both repeatedly to fail and to learn from those failures'

Trying, failing and adjusting is something we learn very early in life. As children learning to walk we did not stand up and walk across the room at the first attempt. We stood, fell, and tried again.

If you have read a number of PMA books then I am sure that you have already heard the story I am about to relate. I will, however, make no apology for repeating it as it illustrates the point of Try, Fail and Adjust very well.

Thomas Edison is reputed to have discovered the key to the electric light bulb on his 1,000th experiment. By that time the people around him were questioning his sanity; but he never doubted himself as, prior to his successful attempt, he told an associate that he had found 999 ways that it did not work.

The highest achievers in this world have had more 'noes' and rejections than the non-achievers. There is a strange myth amongst unsuccessful people that achievers never get rejected, but, when you look at people like Sylvester Stallone, Walt Disney and Edison we can see that this is not true. They simply kept going, overcoming any rejection.

As with Edison, when things do not work the first time, you just have to find another way. Try again and, if that does not work, try again but change your approach; and if that still does not work – guess what – try again, but change your approach!

'when things go wrong, make sure that you do not get into a state of self-sabotage'

When things go wrong, make sure that you do not get into a state of self-sabotage. The way forward is to keep re-adjusting. Do not even think of giving up.

One of the biggest things we must overcome is giving in too early. When things do not go quite our way the easiest thing in the world is to quit. But winners never quit and quitters never win.

It is at times like these when you will need your Perfect Vision. Visualise what type of person you will become if you give up, visualise what will happen to you. If you find yourself trying, failing and then giving up, then it is almost certainly because your aim is not important enough to you. Go back and look at your goals.

'visualise what type of person you will become if you give up, visualise what will happen to you'

On 30th March 1988, I set out with Ian Botham and a number of other walkers to walk 500 miles across the French Alps on the Hannibal Walk, in aid of Leukaemia Research. After the first two days two walkers were forced to pull out of the walk after X-rays showed them to have stress fractures. The remaining walkers were all in pain and discomfort, with swollen and blistered feet, but everyone persisted because our goal was important to us and our minds and bodies soon began to adjust to the discipline.

On one particular day we were due to follow Hannibal's route and take a raft across the River Rhône. It was decided, however, that for the safety of the elephants, we would cross by a bridge further down the river.

The pre-arranged programme was not changed and many of the walkers were saying that we had a day off because we only had six miles to walk that day. Yet, can you imagine walking down to the shops and back for a newspaper, covering a six-mile return trip? Our persistence had paid off and the way our minds were working had changed. To us it was a day off.

When we arrived in Turin on 19th April 1988, the last day, we had walked 33 miles and were taken to a reception that lasted two hours. The walkers were relaxed, strolling around talking to people – a far cry from 21 days before.

Like any change you ever make it takes time and your mind will start to question you. Take one day at a time. As you get nearer your goal, visualise your achievement and do not ever think of quitting.

'even when you think that you have tried absolutely everything, remember that you have not'

Even when you think that you have tried absolutely everything, remember that you have not.

DO NOT FEAR NOES

A lot of people with very little talent have become great achievers and made a very large impact on the world, because they have overcome their fear of rejection.

Many people fear being rejected or being told 'no' and, because of their fear, they never ask. But if you never ask you will never get.

The next time that you are scared to ask for fear of being told 'no' ask yourself what is the very worst thing that can happen.

If the answer is only that someone could say 'no' and reject one of your ideas then ask yourself, 'Can I handle it?' The answer will obviously be 'yes', so ask.

WORK ON WEAKNESSES

One of the major parts of any improvement programme is to work on your weaknesses.

What makes people successful in any sphere of life is that they have found out their weaknesses and worked on them until they have turned them into strengths.

'what makes people successful in any sphere of life is that they have found out their weaknesses and worked on them'

To help you decide the areas on which you need to work make a self-evaluation list, for example 'I am good at . . .', 'I need to improve . . .'.

When listing your weaknesses, also make sure that your belief in yourself stays very positive by listing ten strengths for every three weaknesses. Then have the vision to see how much better you are going to be when you have turned those weaknesses into strengths.

Remember that if someone else has had success then so can you. But also remember that no one becomes a success overnight: you will need a burning desire for achievement coupled with great persistence to make it happen.

'remember that no one becomes a success overnight'

When your weakness eventually becomes a strength, move it across the page into the other column and start work on the next weakness until that column is empty. Then you can add more to your list and so continue on your improvement programme.

One of my favourite stories about turning weaknesses into strengths is about a hunter who is walking through the woods one day on his way back to camp. He hears a rustling in the bushes and as he looks round a lion leaps towards him.

He turns and fires two quick shots but misses the lion on both occasions. Fortunately for the hunter the lion leaps over him. The hunter turns and runs as fast as he can back to camp but all night he lays awake thinking that he must improve his short-range shooting.

'work on your weaknesses until they become strengths'

The next morning, he is throwing cans into the air and practising his shots, when he hears a rustling close by. He parts the leaves to find the cause of the noise and what does he find in the clearing? The same lion practising short jumps!

So, work on your weaknesses until they become strengths.

MAKE THINGS IMPORTANT ENOUGH AND YOU WILL GET THE RESULTS

When a child comes home from school and gets seven out of ten, although it means that the child has made some mistakes, we should obviously congratulate and motivate him. However, if we carried that philosophy through to adulthood, and the adult became a pilot or a midwife, then we would not consider seven out of ten landings acceptable or seven out of ten babies that were not dropped on their head a reasonable standard.

In the main we do just enough to get by, but, when something is important enough to us we take extra care and do not make mistakes. Make sure that what you are doing is important enough to you and you will get the results you desire.

'make sure that what you are doing is important enough to you and you will get the results you desire'

AVOID MEDIOCRITY

In order to be an achiever we must avoid mediocrity at all costs. There are too many average people in this world. So make sure that you never settle for mediocrity in anything that you do.

Start to think 'big' and raise the level of your performance. The better your performance, the more effective and successful you are certain to be.

'we must avoid mediocrity at all costs'

Keep a high expectation and commitment to your success programme and keep highly motivated to strive for excellence and superior performance while completing any task.

DO NOT WASTE TIME

Something which we all have in common is a time account. This is unlike a bank account in that we cannot add to it and we cannot get a balance from it. We can only withdraw another 24 hours from our account each day. With this in mind we must place greater value on how we spend our time; after all we do not know how much we have left.

However, in my business, as in many others, we work on monthly targets and it would be impossible for me to say how many times I have heard people say, 'I've had a bad month'. But let us assume that we died at the age of 70 – that is only 840 months from birth to death.

Top achievers recognise that they might have the odd bad moment but life is far too short to have a bad month. So remember, if things do not go the way you want, you should adjust immediately and make sure you do not waste time.

'do not muddle activity with achievement'

Successful people seem to have a lot more time than unsuccessful people because they organise it properly and concentrate on what is important. However, do not muddle activity with achievement. Ask yourself whether you are efficient and effective. Goal achievers are both.

Avoid trivia and do not waste time. Question whether what you are doing is important and whether it is getting you closer to, or further from, your goal.

One of the key things to do is to write down a list of priorities. Make sure that you start each day with a 'to do' list and complete each task one by one in strict order of priority. In that way, anything which does not get done is the least important.

You will come across many time wasters who are non-achievers. Allow them to waste their time but do not allow them to waste yours. Time is very valuable and if you waste time you murder success.

One of the biggest wastes of time is shuffling paper. You see people in offices who pick up the same piece of paper time and time again but never deal with it. I challenge you never to touch the same piece of paper twice. Pick it up and deal with it.

LEARN TO LISTEN

'time is very valuable and if you waste time you murder success'

I am sure that you have heard people say many times, 'I have a bad memory for names'. Yet, I am sure that if I asked you to list the names of your parents, your brothers and sisters, aunts and uncles you would have instant recall.

How many times have you been to a party and been introduced to someone only to find that within minutes you are unable to recall their name?

It is not that you have a bad memory, it is merely that we hear but we do not listen. The fact remains that it is not possible to remember what you have not learned in the first place.

So the very next time you are introduced to somebody, make a point of checking that you have correctly heard the name and associate it with something which will help you to recall it in the future. The phrase, 'I have a bad memory', will become a thing of the past.

GET THE RIGHT TEAM AROUND YOU

One of the most vital ingredients for success is to get the right team around you in your home and business life. We must surround ourselves with individuals who are highly motivated and share our desire for achievement.

We have all heard people say phrases like, 'How did they get themselves into that mess?' or 'How did that happen?' Very often it is because we fail to take notice of warning signs and go into personal or business partnerships with the wrong person. Take extra care.

To be successful, you must ensure that you have the right team around you. When considering entering into a marriage or business partnership, I would personally suggest that you consider very carefully with whom you are going to spend the rest of your life. Tying the knot, whether in your personal or business life, is a lot easier than untying it.

'we must surround ourselves with individuals who are highly motivated and share our desire for achievement'

When choosing your partner, be sure that you both share a common aim and goal in life. Both partners have to be motivated and pull together, otherwise the partnership begins to falter and time is spent on mending fences rather than building bridges. Do not spend time on endless arguments that achieve little. With Perfect Vision you will realise that you do not have the time.

The wrong partner in business can totally destroy you. You must get to know with whom you are developing your career. It is no use climbing a ladder only to discover, when you get to the top, that it has been leaning up against the wrong wall.

Very often in business, individuals offer incentives and 'golden hellos' to try to recruit people into the company. Do not allow yourself to be bought merely for short-term gain. In any partnership join only because of the future career opportunities it offers.

In both cases have a very good look at the bride, not the wedding presents.

'have a very good look at the bride, not the wedding presents'

FOLLOW THE RIGHT LEADER

We now obviously realise that our environment is very important to us and it is essential in any improvement programme to follow the right leader. In following a leader, find someone who is currently doing what you most want to do and is doing it extremely well.

Following a leader immediately removes a large barrier. You realise that if he can, so can you and if he has been successful then, if you can copy his example, you will attain the same results.

Take, as an example, Dr Roger Bannister, the first person to run a four-minute mile. When he achieved this he not only became the first person to complete a mile in under four minutes but he also removed the conditioning in the minds of other athletes that had held them back in the past. They recognised by his achievement that if he could do it, so could they. Within a matter of weeks John Michael Landy was the next to break the barrier.

At Harlow, in August 1989, at one of the six events which General Portfolio sponsored for Leukaemia Research, Peter Elliott ran the fastest mile that year – in just 3.53 minutes. It was obviously a tremendous achievement, but, in many ways, something equally incredible but less remarked upon was the fact that the next seven runners also beat the four-minute barrier. In following the leader they had also attained outstanding results.

The following year Peter again ran another 'Miles of Miles' race, at Battersea Park, in which he completed the mile in 3.51 minutes. Again, seven competitors finished in under four minutes.

As we have said earlier in this book, we have been conditioned to think about what we cannot do. But we can do anything if someone has done it before us. By following a leader, we can concentrate all our energies on completing the task rather than questioning whether it can be done.

'following the right leader will help ensure the attainment of our desired results'

So following the right leader will help ensure the attainment of our desired results; but be warned, following the wrong leader can be more damaging than not following a leader at all.

When picking your leader be selective. Ask yourself, 'If I were he, how would I be?', 'If I were she, how would I be?'

Success is caught not taught, so select a creative leader; a person, who your vision tells you can, if you follow their actions, help you to get similar results.

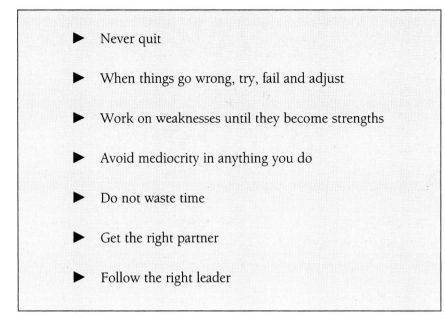

- ▶ Never quit

- ▶ When things go wrong, try, fail and adjust

- ▶ Work on weaknesses until they become strengths

- ▶ Avoid mediocrity in anything you do

- ▶ Do not waste time

- ▶ Get the right partner

- ▶ Follow the right leader

KEY POINTS TO PERFECT VISION

❝Like life, boxing can be very hard work. If you want to be successful at boxing you have to have an incredible amount of commitment. Not only do you need it to motivate yourself to go through the hours of hard training in the gym and on the roads, but also when you finally get into the ring.❞

FRANK BRUNO

❝I don't think that it is a bad thing to say, 'I have had a bad game but it is done and now I am going to come back and have two good games'. It is a positive way of thinking. If you had the choice of someone saying to you, 'Would you rather lose and be disappointed, but know that you are going to become better for it, or not lose at all?', I know which I would choose.❞

JOHN BARNES

❝You have different types of disappointment when you lose. If you lose and you've played well, a certain part of you is pleased you played well. If you've lost and you've played badly, you're more distraught. But the depression lasts for a very short amount of time. If I have a bad match it doesn't sadden me for very long before I'm looking to the next one, working towards that. I always look on the more positive side of improving if I've done badly.❞

STEVE DAVIS

– 10 –

BECOME

'you will now no doubt have discovered for yourself the power of using your vision'

At the beginning of this book I asked you to trust me and I am sure that by now you are delighted that you took my advice. You will now no doubt have discovered for yourself the power of using your vision and running a programme for success. Using these formulas you will live life with purpose. You are on the road to *'Being the best you can possibly be'*.

But this is not the end, it is just the beginning. Whatever level you have achieved so far, this formula will continue to work with absolutely no limits. You can either be a better cook or go as far as becoming a Cordon Bleu chef – how far you go in your chosen field is up to you.

You will, however, continue to develop as an individual. You will continue your growth and will start to be recognised as one of those people who are now creating their life exactly as they visualised and wanted it to be.

SO WHAT COULD GO WRONG?

Two of the main reasons for people not being continually successful in life are ignorance and complacency. We now have the system that works so that we have removed ignorance. However, as you develop, remember that success is a journey not a destiny and you must have the constant urge to improve and advance every single day.

'success is a journey not a destiny'

I am sure that you have wondered why so many successful individuals who have made it to the top of their fields suddenly lose all that they have achieved. Why so many seemingly unstoppable people end up with so little.

The answer is simple. They forgot one of the golden rules for success and that is to never stop doing what got them there in the first place.

'never stop doing what got you there in the first place'

The major reason why companies get into difficulties is because the competent people who have achieved success in the past stop doing what created that original success. They become complacent.

Make sure that you do not become one of the individuals who stop growing by not continuing to do the things which made you successful, or you could find that you may well be one of today's successes who quickly becomes one of tomorrow's failures.

However, so long as you constantly practise the art of visualisation your horizons will expand. You will not have the time to become complacent because the more that you obtain personal satisfaction and monetary wealth, the more you will increase your understanding of what is available to you.

BECOMING A LEADER

Seeing people who have achieved through using the **Visualise – Think – Believe – Act – Become** success principles always compels me to pass on my message to others.

'share your ideas, so that others can discover the pleasures you have found'

When you continue to work the system which has helped you to success, the people around you will see that success and want to emulate you. Whilst you will continue to develop and grow, they will begin to follow you. You will have become a leader.

Make sure, then, that you share your ideas, so that others can discover the pleasures you have found.

On any improvement programme, however, our achievements are all relative. Whilst you will be a leader in certain fields you will continue to be a follower in others. So make sure that, when you are a leader you lead with vision and inspiration and when you are a follower be absolutely certain that you follow a leader who will help you obtain your objectives and aims.

'live life on purpose, developing and growing as an individual every single day'

THE FUTURE LOOKS GREAT!

You can now take control of your life by using your vision, goal planning and programming to create everything you have ever dreamed about. Remember the compounding effect. Changes lead to more changes and personal development will lead you to more personal development.

Live life on purpose, developing and growing as an individual every single day. Spend your time goal achieving and then you will face each day with much more energy and excitement.

It will take a tremendous amount of energy and effort to succeed and go on. At times it will seem like there are not enough hours in a day, but keep your vision of the person you wish to become and you will be rewarded for your efforts.

Keep your vision focused on the future but do not shift everything there at the expense of today. You must get the balance right. Live today to the full, as if it were your last, but lay the groundwork for a fantastic future. You can have both.

This can be obtained with a clearly defined programme. Once you have devised the plan to organise your time for living today and creating your tomorrows, make sure that you enthusiastically and consistently take heavy action on your programme.

Get totally committed to your own personal excellence because, of all the people you will ever know, you are the only one you neither leave nor lose. Make sure that you become **'The Best You Can Possibly Be'**.

'get totally committed to your own personal excellence'

I will not wish you luck – you can make your own.

Whatever you perfectly visualise, really believe, strongly desire, run a programme to achieve and then enthusiastically act upon must, inevitably, become yours.

ACKNOWLEDGEMENTS

First and foremost I should like to thank everyone at General Portfolio for helping me both to formulate my views and to put them into practice.

I very much appreciate the contributions of John Barnes, Ian Botham, Frank Bruno, Steve Davis, Peter Elliott, Allison Fisher, Steve Perryman and Robert Swan. I am grateful to all of them for being more than willing to reveal some of the secrets of their success and for making time available in their extraordinarily busy schedules.

Thanks also, to Douglas Osborne of the Leukaemia Research Fund for writing the Foreword for this book.

I should like to thank Sonny Peart for his collaboration on a long list of articles that have provided some of the backbone for *Perfect Vision*; to Claire Costello for her excellent illustrations; to Nigel Cooke, Marketing Director of General Portfolio, Brendan Foster, Eric Wilkins and Dave Roberts of Nova International, for their enthusiasm for the idea of a book and their assistance with its publication; and to George Goodwin of George Goodwin PR, for helping to make things happen.

Last, and by no means least, special thanks to Jane Ducarreaux, who has acted as my shadow over the last couple of months. She has done far more than just transcribe my words; she has worked extremely hard, to a very short deadline, to organise the book. She has offered a wide range of helpful advice and, above all, even when presented with yet another late "improvement", has been unfailingly good-humoured throughout.

January 1991

AUTHOR PROFILE

Bob Patmore has come through careers in professional football and music to become National Sales Manager of General Portfolio Financial Planning Services, one of the leading financial planning groups in the country.

Between 1963 and 1970 he was carving out a career in football, playing for Tottenham Hotspur, Luton, Watford and Cambridge United. But then, realising that he would never play for his country, he moved away from football and into a career in music.

He spent the next three years recording and touring Switzerland and America with his band. Returning home from an American tour he decided that 'it was time to make some serious money' and started on the career which was to lead him to the top of his profession and his status as a multi-millionaire.

Under his guidance, General Portfolio's sales force has grown from 400 to over 3,500 in under five years and his personal philosophy has helped others in the pursuit of their own excellence.

He is heavily involved with the company's fund-raising for the Leukaemia Research Fund, completed the Hannibal Walk with Ian Botham in 1988 and, after many years persuasion, has written *Perfect Vision* to further help boost the finances of the Fund.